Who was Kit Marlowe?

DELLA HILTON

WHO WAS KIT MARLOWE?

The story of the poet and playwright

Taplinger Publishing Company
New York

First published in the United States in 1977 by
TAPLINGER PUBLISHING CO., INC.
Copyright © 1977 by Della Hilton

Printed in Great Britain

Library of Congress Catalog Card Number: 76-53911

ISBN 0-8008-8291-1

To Myra Roper, for bringing
literary distinction to
Melbourne University

Contents

Illustrations

Introduction

Who was Christopher Marlowe? For me, when I first heard his 'divine Zenocrate' speech as a seventeen-year-old schoolgirl, he was the greatest poet in the English language. The following year, when I studied *Tamburlaine* at university, he was the most exciting of the early playwrights.

I was fortunate because I met the real Marlowe before I heard the myth. *Tamburlaine*, which was published in his lifetime, is true Marlowe, as is his mature and less bombastic *Edward II*. The partially corrupt texts of *The Jew of Malta, The Massacre at Paris* and *Doctor Faustus* still tell us more of their author than the rumour and speculation which has grown up round him.

Much is actually known about Marlowe – more than about his contemporary Shakespeare – because he can be traced through the records of his school and university, at Canterbury, and in London where he was involved with two definable circles, that of his patron Thomas Walsingham and, to a lesser degree, Raleigh's School of Night.

These facts must be viewed in the light of his writings if we are to have a true picture of the man; too often Marlowe's plays are read or produced with alleged hindsight, which attributes false meanings to otherwise straightforward passages. For example, Marlowe is described as 'violent' when his record, set beside that of contemporaries, is relatively mild and his plays are no more bloodthirsty than the fashion of the time. The label 'atheist' came very early, from a jealous playwright; and though this playwright misquoted, saying that Tamburlaine 'dared God from Heaven' when he actually dared Mohammed, the mistake has still contributed to the myth. Marlowe was outspoken and a challenging thinker, as were all Raleigh's School of Night, most of whom were also accused of atheism, but present-day biographers of Raleigh, for example, have put this in perspective, while Marlowe is still cloaked in unnecessary speculation. Hearsay criticisms of Raleigh receive closer scrutiny than those of Marlowe.

Another subject of speculation is Marlowe's alleged homosexuality. This is based on two passages from his works, which have fewer homosexual characters and descriptions than those of some contemporaries, and two flippant hearsay comments quoted by a detractor. The detractor claimed that Marlowe said 'that St John the Evangelist was bedfellow to C(hrist) and leaned alwaies in his bosome, that he used him as the sinners of Sodoma' and that 'all they that love not Tobacco and Boies were fooles'. In the first Christ is condemned for supposed homosexuality like the 'sinners of Sodoma', and the second seems to link homosexuality with the new diversion of pipe smoking taken up by Raleigh's circle, hinting that a number of people did both. Those accusing Marlowe of homosexuality often omit the first allegation and merely quote the second; the translations of Ovid's love poetry and the erotic parts of *Hero and Leander* are overlooked.

Perhaps some people wish Marlowe, like Shakespeare, to stay a mystery, but too much is known about him for a true picture of the man not to be given.

Much harm has been done to Marlowe by those who suggest he wrote Shakespeare's plays, because this makes him seem an interloper, when he was a great playwright on his own account.

In recognizing that Marlowe was not the writer of Shakespeare's plays some people mistakenly dismiss him altogether, thus diminishing our literary canon, and denying Marlowe his historical importance in the development of drama. Marlowe, in fact, was the pioneer and Shakespeare followed his example.

Others, since the revelation that Marlowe had done some spying, concentrate on the Man of Action, and give little attention to his writings.

My book aims to give the life of Marlowe as it was, from the facts, documents, and in the light of his writings.

What emerges is the life of a brilliant, attractive and sometimes disturbing man; and also a picture of the period, one of the most exciting in our history, when the Spanish Armada was defeated and English literature flourished.

There are some people who have not heard of Christopher Marlowe, and wonder why there is interest in this man who lived four hundred years ago.

This book is also for them. Marlowe's colourful life and transcendent poetry is part of the heritage of all English-speaking people.

For their assistance I wish to thank: Dr William Urry, ex-Canterbury archivist and now Ceremonial Dean of the Modern History Faculty at Oxford, to whom the Marlowe family is as real as if they were his next-door neighbours; A. J. P. Taylor, for sympathetic and valuable guidance in preparing this biography; Peter Pollak of Marlowe House, King's School, Canterbury; Christopher Falkus and John Curtis for encouragement; George MacBeth for poetry help; Dr Christopher Andrew of Corpus Christi, Cambridge; the Rev. Canon C. Norwood of Sutton Valence, Kent, and Southchurch; archivist Katharine Wheeler; Dr Christopher Wrigley; the reference librarian of the Paddington branch of the Westminster Library; and my family and a number of friends for sympathetic listening. All Marlowe quotations have been taken from the Penguin editions.

1 · Canterbury

Christopher Marlowe was born in Canterbury in February 1564, two months earlier than Shakespeare whom he was to precede to London. Canterbury at this time was a thriving market town, as well as the possessor of England's premier cathedral. Its industry had benefited from the settling there of French and Dutch Huguenots, who had escaped the Catholic persecutions. Marlowe's *The Massacre at Paris*, about the slaughter of Protestants in Paris on St Bartholomew's Day in 1572, drew on information from these people and from his later visit(s) to France.

Christopher's father, John Marlowe, was a shoemaker. He employed apprentices, was a Freeman of the City and was active in civic affairs – the sort of man who would stand surety for another's debts and forget to pay his own. His wife Katherine came from Dover. Little else of importance is known of her except that she had a relative who was a Doctor of Divinity. She, rather than John Marlowe – whose rumbustious nature is clear from the legal affrays he was involved in – was anxious to further Kit's education. Eventually Kit was awarded a scholarship to King's School, the famous public school adjacent to Canterbury Cathedral that was to give him his pre-university education.

When another male child survived (Kit had two small brothers who died) he became a choirboy, probably again at Mistress Marlowe's instigation. The five sisters who from Canterbury records appear rather unruly, settled in their native town.

Childhood in Canterbury was not much different from today. Boys played in the ruins of St Augustine's Abbey and in the streets. On an outing into the country they saw orchards, green lanes and tall trees. Church bells pealed, including the great medieval bell Sanctus Georgius, which has since been destroyed in an air raid. They were sent to church regularly while their fathers – like John Marlowe the shoemaker, and Plessington the baker (an emigrant from Cheshire) – went less frequently. They had elementary lessons and some, like Christopher, ultimately became Masters of Arts. Others could not sign their names.

Some of John Marlowe's apprentices were lively lads, causing entertainment for the Marlowe sisters, pain for Kit, and consternation for his mother and father. Two of them – Richard Umberfield and Lactantius Preston – were mentioned in legal records, one for seducing a girl and one for fighting. Another, William Hughes, was later thought by Lord Alfred Douglas to be Mr W. H. of Shakespeare's Sonnets. As Canterbury's streets were crowded with markets, were still within city walls, and had buildings almost meeting overhead, young Kit would have had little peace. It is no wonder that he became a dreamer. The flights of fancy in his first play about Tamburlaine, whom he could have read about in the King's School Master's library, were an escape and an ambition for him.

His feeling for colour, demonstrated particularly in *Tamburlaine*, was heightened by looking at the stained glass during the numerous church services he attended. The Canterbury stained glass of the period, some of which survives, was very beautiful.

> The crystal springs, whose taste illuminates,
> Refined eyes with an eternal sight,
> Like tried silver run through Paradise . . .
> (*Tamburlaine*, Part Two, Act II)

pictures the effect of sun shining through a stained-glass window.

In her will his mother also shows an awareness of colour, particularly in the description of what she left to her daughters. Kit's wish to protect her from the daughters' unruly behaviour can be imagined. Kit returned home for visits from both Cambridge and London – his only extant signature, for example, is as witness to a neighbour's will when he was visiting Canterbury in November 1585.

One of John Marlowe's daughters was in trouble in Canterbury for blasphemy, as Dr William Urry discovered in the Canterbury archives. Kit earned his reputation later in London – except for one affray when he visited Canterbury from London in 1592. His father, it is interesting to note, became more respectable as he grew older – though he still sometimes neglected to pay his bills.

In Elizabethan times 'Marlowe' was spelt in various ways. At Cambridge Christopher was 'Marlin', 'Marlen', 'Marley', 'Marly', 'Marlyn', 'Marlye' and 'Merling'; and he entered King's School as 'Marley'.

He may have received tuition at King's School before he was awarded his scholarship there, as his uncle Thomas Arthur, who was unmarried till the time Kit received the scholarship, may have previously paid for his nephew to be a day scholar. Kit was almost fifteen when he took up his scholarship on 14 January in the Michaelmas term of 1578–9.

King's School was the oldest public school in England. Henry VIII had intervened in 1541 to grant a charter to the dean and chapter which provided for masters, an usher and fifty scholars who were to eat at the common table. The statutes specified that the fifty boys should be 'destitute of the help of friends, and endowed with minds apt for learning, who shall be called scholars of the grammar school, and shall be sustained out of the funds of our Church'. Though Kit was by no means destitute some of the scholars were even less so, as gentlemen's sons were given preference.

Some actually wore shoes made by Kit's father – a few bills of John Marlowe the shoemaker from this time still exist. Perhaps the picture of Bajazeth in a cage, which was in the library, and which was later used in *Tamburlaine*, impressed Kit because he wished to treat similarly boys who were contemptuous of his father's menial status!

Lessons at King's School began at six in the morning with a

3

religious service and ended with another service at five in the afternoon. Then there was 'prep'. It was a long day for the boys.

They received a yearly allowance for 'commons' – food, and money to pay for two and a half yards of cloth for a new gown at Christmas. The total was £4. Christopher Marley was listed in the cathedral treasurer's accounts for 1578-9 as receiving quarterly payments of £1.

Christopher's life was broadened by his scholarship to King's School, particularly as he studied in attractive buildings. The great hall of the school, a survival from a monastery, was next to a statuesque Norman staircase. The spacious cathedral cloisters through which he walked each day can still be seen. In these surroundings he studied Latin, the classics, oratory, scripture and works of relatively modern scholars like Erasmus. Plays were produced, but usually in Latin. The difference between his studies in this environment and the hustle and informality of his father's shop was striking. The standard of conversation of his sisters, the apprentices, and his parents was on a noticeably lower level than that of the King's School boys with their masters. And there was considerably more space available for the boys at King's School, compared with the shoemaker's crowded household.

One of Marlowe's sisters, Margaret, was gentle and became the 'respectable' member of the family, marrying a worthy citizen and settling peaceably in Canterbury. In *The Jew of Malta*, Barabas's daughter Abigail, who is portrayed as an appealing human being, compared with the shadowy idealized Zenocrate of his earlier play *Tamburlaine*, may have been based on Margaret. There are echoes of Canterbury in *The Jew of Malta*, and even descriptions of the Kent countryside, which are otherwise present only in *Arden of Faversham* – a play probably, though not certainly, by Marlowe.

The street markets of Canterbury influenced his choice of Tamburlaine as a subject for drama, since though Tamburlaine became a mighty conquerer, he began as a shepherd. The rise of a man such as he saw bringing sheep to market, to world tyrant, appealed to a boy who read these exciting stories in the Master's library at King's School. He later used pastoral imagery, and was referred to as 'dead shepherd' by Shakespeare in *As You Like It*.

A line in *The Jew of Malta* – 'There's a dark entry where they take it in' – recalls the name given to the passage between King's School and the cathedral cloisters through Prior Sellingegate, which the pupils often used. Christopher heard stories associated with it, and certainly this passage is mentioned later in the *Ingoldsby Legends*; it was the place where the monks buried Nell Cook after she had served the canon with poisoned pie, and was sufficiently atmospheric to give rise to many stories. In *The Jew of Malta* Barabas's servant takes a pot of poisoned broth into the nunnery through the dark entry, killing all the nuns, including his daughter.

If Marlowe did base Barabas's daughter Abigail on his sister Margaret it was for similar personality, not story. Nevertheless, five noisy sisters might have suggested to him how trying life would be in a nunnery.

Medieval Canterbury was a city of narrow streets and haphazard buildings, with little lanes running between or behind them. The thin river Stour was flanked by houses, including those of Huguenot weavers; some still stand today. There was a ducking-seat for misdoers at Hoppers Mill. Between two houses was a wall with a hole like that used by Pyramis and Thisbe in Shakespeare's *A Midsummer Night's Dream*. Busy Mercery Lane, leading up to the Christchurch Gate of the cathedral, held traders including George Ansell the grocer. Other streets held markets. The gate itself is impressive, bearing coats of arms, figures and decorations. Once inside the gate, the calm of the cathedral absorbs a person. Christopher felt this difference when he returned to King's School from the shoemaker's shop – the bustle disappeared and the new atmosphere enveloped him. It is unlikely that Cambridge University had been considered for John Marlowe's son, but Kit's ability, and confidence increased by education in the Cathedral close, added a new dimension to his ambition.

In 1580 he received a Dr Matthew Parker scholarship to Corpus Christi College at Cambridge University.

Dr Matthew Parker, Archbishop of Canterbury from 1558 to 1575, had previously been Master of Corpus Christi from 1544 to 1553, and in 1575 he made a will endowing three scholarships to the college of £3.6s.8d. per annum each, one specifically for a King's School scholar born in Canterbury. Christopher received this, and planned to emulate his relative by becoming a Doctor of Divinity. At seventeen he was quite old to go to Cambridge because undergraduates were often as young as fourteen. (His scholarship to King's School had also been late.)

There was an interesting proficiency stipulation for holders of Matthew Parker scholarships. 'All which schollers shall and must at the time of their election be so entered into the skill of song as that they shall at first sight solf and sing plaine song. And they shalbe of the best and aptest schollers well instructed in their gramer and if it may be such as can make a verse.' Christopher could certainly 'make a verse'.

The mixed feelings of his family when Christopher was awarded his Cambridge scholarship can be imagined: pride, sadness because he was going away, perhaps envy. An honour for John Marlowe, and the indignity of being wrong about his son's ability – if he had been wrong, which seems likely.

Christopher's clothes had to be prepared and food baked by Mistress Marlowe for him to take. He would be excited and perhaps nervous about the journey from Canterbury to Cambridge. He was to travel by wagon to the Thames estuary, and thence to Cambridge. A long journey in 1580, and a dark one in November and December. Though Pashley, whom Christopher was to succeed, would not relinquish the scholarship till the springtime of the next year, the trip was to be made before Christmas. Christopher would settle and accustom himself to the new life.

He was already prepared for writing. Among the books he had access to at King's School were Fortescue's *Foreste*, Loniceros's *Chronica Turcica* and Munster's *Cosmography*, all containing

6

source material for *Tamburlaine*. *Cosmography* particularly inspired a boy at this time when the land discoveries by English sailors were exciting enquiring minds. He was later to meet the explorer Walter Raleigh. Kit was to find another well-stocked library at Corpus Christi, but King's School laid a solid foundation. There was also time to meditate at King's School, and, apart from the books, Kit found the music inspiring – for example, in *Tamburlaine*:

> The cherubins and Holy seraphins,
> That sing and play before the King of Kings,
> Use all their voices, and their instruments
> To entertain divine Zenocrate:
> And in this sweet and curious harmony,
> The god that tunes this music to our souls
> Holds out his hands in highest majesty
> To entertain divine Zenocrate.

This passage begins 'Now walk the angels on the walls of heaven', describing a painting in Canterbury Cathedral which has an angel walking on a heavenly mount.

The Canterbury Kit was leaving was a community of 4,000 souls, containing a great variety of people. It had been a gathering place for pilgrims to Becket's tomb until twenty-five years before, and was still a centre for refugees and travellers because of its position on the main road from Dover to London. The Cambridge for which he was destined was a distinguished, homogeneous city. While he probably considered Cambridge the more congenial, Canterbury had given him a picture of human nature unrivalled for comprehensiveness. Though his first play, *Tamburlaine*, was idealized, his later works drew on the human characteristics he observed in Canterbury's mixed population.

Since the Marlowe household had moved several times because of non-payment of rent, when Kit was accepted for Cambridge University gossip may have suggested that his family had ideas above their station. It says much for Elizabethan education that scholarships were available for brilliant pupils like Kit.

When the departure day dawned and he was taken to board the wagon outside the Saracen's Head, the family was watched by interested neighbours and bystanders; some no doubt wished him luck, while his sisters and his mother wept, and his father, if he were true to character, blustered. Kit's clothes were tied in a handkerchief, his food in another, and he had a bag of books. The final parting as he stepped aboard the wagon was emotional – to travel to Cambridge, but to leave his family and Canterbury. Then the wagon drove through the city gates, into the Kent countryside.

The journey was long and uncomfortable. In the springtime it would have been beautiful, with apple and cherry orchards in bloom, wild flowers, and trees breaking into pale green leaf. But in December the trees were starkly bare, and the roads rutted and muddy. Few other travellers were on the road, and the villages through which they passed had candles in the windows and smoke pouring from the chimneys.

Where Kit's wagon crossed the Thames estuary is not known as there were ferries at several points, but wherever he crossed he had his first view of London spires from there. Six and a half years later he was to arrive in London with *Tamburlaine*, Part One, and cause a sensation. Much was to happen first.

2 · Cambridge

Christopher reached Corpus Christi on 10 December 1580. He bought a drink costing one penny – expensive for a youth with £3. 6s. 8d. per year to live on. He had his own food which his mother had packed for his first meals at Corpus Christi.

Arriving early, Kit was in time for the Christmas services, ceremonies and concerts, and he had leisure to adjust to the new surroundings. King's School had partially prepared him, but his father's shop had always been nearby. Now the university was his constant environment.

The university colleges did not flank the river Cam as the Canterbury buildings did the Stour. Between the colleges and the river were green banks, stretches of lawn and open spaces. The sky was not cluttered by roofs and chimneys as Canterbury's had been, and Christopher discovered 'the fiery spangled veil' of the stars.

> In the silence of thy solemn evening's walk,
> Making the mantle of the richest night,
> The moon, the planets and the meteors, light,

he wrote of Zenocrate in *Tamburlaine*, Part One. Arts students studied some astronomy in their first year, and this, combined with his vision of open skies, made an impression on Kit. He made much use of cosmic imagery in *Tamburlaine*.

The Corpus Christi library had a wide range of books about Timur the Lame's conquests, and Kit probably began to write *Tamburlaine*, Part One, before he succeeded to his scholarship, when he had time to read and write freely. Books by authors like Perondius and Mexia, and Ortelius's large atlas of the world, helped him to chart Tamburlaine's battles in detail. The fact that some of the geographical information is wrong is a reflection of contemporary beliefs, not of Kit's inaccuracy. Writing *Tamburlaine* helped him to adapt to his university surroundings by providing creative work to build his confidence.

When he left to go to London in 1587, Part One was finished and he had made notes for Part Two, which he completed in time for staging some months later. And while he studied for his degree he incorporated work on *Tamburlaine* and his various poetry translations into his daily routine. During the first weeks at Corpus he also probably began his translations of Ovid. A finely illustrated Latin copy of Ovid's *Elegies* was available to encourage him.

His new home was a refitted storeroom facing on to a courtyard. Now called the Old Court, a plaque commemorates his residence there. Several other people shared the 'chamber' during his six years, and one, Thomas Lewgar, was there for all this period. Thomas Lewgar was less restless than spirited Kit, and his complementariness may have been the reason for their surviving friendship. The chamber was furnished with essentials like chairs, tables, beds with bolsters of feathers, and chests for their clothes. At night they worked by candlelight. Bells for chapel woke them in the early morning.

Regulations at Cambridge were strict, though often disregarded. By rights students should not patronize taverns, fairs or entertainments like those put on by strolling players, unless accompanied by members of the college. They wore ankle-length straight woollen gowns of black or brown, though some rich men's sons sported velvets of bright colours, ruffs and even swords. These sprigs not only frequented the inns, but indulged in card-playing, dice, and sports like cock-fighting and bearbaiting.

In term time, a day at Corpus Christi was more arduous than that of King's School. Bells called scholars to chapel at 5 a.m. for an hour's service. Breakfast was at six. Lectures followed – in the first year students studied rhetoric and some Greek, arithmetic and astronomy. Dinner was at noon. The next two hours were devoted to 'disputations' and discussions, which often took place in Latin or Hebrew. They then read freely and studied alone. There was also a chapel service in the evening.

According to the terms of Kit's allowance he was to receive his 'barber and his launder freely without anything paying therefore', which helped to save both money and time. Hair was supposed to be worn short without 'long locks' hanging from the head, though this regulation was not always obeyed.

A portrait discovered at the Master's Lodge at Corpus Christi in 1953, marked 'Ætatis suae 21 1585' (aged twenty-one, 1585), shows fairly short hair with no dangling locks. This portrait may be of Christopher Marlowe, as he was twenty-one in 1585, and had recently received his Bachelor of Arts degree, which could have been the occasion of its painting. The costume, however, is richer than Kit would have been expected to wear.

The strongest argument in favour of this being Marlowe's portrait rests on the inscription 'Quod me nutrit me destruit' ('That which nourishes me destroys me'), which is twice referred to by Shakespeare. One reference is in *Pericles*, Act II, scene ii ('Quod me alit me extinguit'), and the other, more significantly, in Sonnet 73; and as Marlowe was the 'other poet' of the Sonnets* this does have a ring of truth about it (though it would be better placed as Sonnet 88 in the sequence if it were following Kit's life chronologically):

> ... In me thou seest the glowing of such fire,
> That on the ashes of his youth doth lie,
> As the death-bed, whereon it must expire,
> Consum'd with that which it was nourish'd by.

A mystery about the references by Shakespeare to 'Quod me nutrit me destruit', if they are about the portrait, is how he knew of its existence. One suggestion is that the portrait (which

---

* See Chapter 15.

now hangs in the dining-room of Corpus Christi) was commissioned by Thomas Walsingham, who was to become the liaison agent for Kit's government service and his poetry patron.

This presupposes that Kit already knew Thomas Walsingham in 1585. The portrait could have been given to Corpus Christi after Kit became famous, and if it had been in the possession of Thomas Walsingham Shakespeare might have heard of it.

Another possibility is that the inscription was added to the portrait when it was given to Corpus Christi after Christopher's death, and was the choice of his friends. It might have been suggested by Shakespeare's poem.

When Kit took up his scholarship in 1581 there was little sign that his career would be much different from those of his colleagues. His record for collecting the weekly shilling allowance paid shows him attending regularly in his first years. He no doubt read more widely than his curriculum needed, but as some students did no work at all, reading widely was an advantageous 'fault'.

The latter part of the sixteenth century was an exciting time to study at a university. The new learning of the Renaissance had broadened erudition from the narrower topics of the Middle Ages. The strictly spiritual virtues had given way to the rediscovery and glorification of man. Painting gained perspective and its subjects humanity. The naked form was no longer sinful, and was painted and sculpted. The argument that Marlowe's detailed description of Leander's body in his poem *Hero and Leander* shows homosexual tendencies falls down in this context. The Renaissance had made the human body a work of art and worthy of such description. Relationships between humans were also explored in depth, and this development made the new drama, of which Kit was to be a great exponent, possible. His play *Edward II* shows the relationship between Gaveston and Edward, Edward and Queen Isabella, and Queen Isabella and Mortimer, and the depth of feeling between Edward and Gaveston is the third side of a balanced triangle. Such an extension of human relationships was justified in the era of learning about man.

In its way *Tamburlaine* was an adolescent hymn to the possibilities of man. A humble shepherd became a great conqueror. Nothing stopped him until, at the end of Part Two, he was overcome by death, and even then he tried to defy it by ordering it to go away.

Kit Marlowe's translations of Ovid's poem are an exploration of the senses.

> In summer's heat and mid-time of the day
> To rest my limbs upon a bed I lay . . .
> Then came Corinna in a long loose gown,
> Her white neck hid with tresses hanging down . . .
> What arms and shoulders did I touch and see,
> How apt her breasts were to be press'd by me . . .
> Judge you the rest; being tir'd she bade me kiss;
> Jove send me more such afternoons as this!
>
> (Book I, Elegia v)

There is a world of difference between translating such a secular Roman poet, and the idealized writings of pre-Renaissance times. While poets of the Middle Ages had their bawdy stories, like some of Chaucer's *Canterbury Tales*, Ovid's sensuous, worldly poetry treated the body with some reverence. The Renaissance began with the rediscovery of classical writing, and Marlowe's translations of Ovid, and later Lucan and Virgil, are in the mainstream of the English re-awakening.

It is not surprising that Ovid was the classical poet who drew the interest of an adolescent poet like Kit. It was much easier to imagine the experiences he described than to seek them. And Ovid's ironic style appealed to students.

The influence of the Reformation had been as telling as that of the Renaissance. By the 1580s Protestantism was split between the orthodox Church of England (of which the Queen was head) and Puritanism; anti-Catholicism had been strengthened by the enmity of Catholic Spain to England. Kit Marlowe had been baptized in his Church of England parish in Canterbury, and had been educated under the shadow of England's greatest cathedral. He was, until the end of his Cambridge years, destined for the Church, holding a scholarship endowed by a previous Archbishop of Canterbury. Before he became suspected of the crime of 'atheism' (usually meaning agnosticism) he was gaining a reputation for outspokenness and uninhibited enquiring. And he was never averse to making jokes about priests and monks, particularly in *The Jew of Malta*.

At Cambridge there are no examples of Christopher being criticized by the authorities until his 'spy' trip to Rheims. Nevertheless he was probably one of the students who objected to attending so many church services; some students actually misbehaved in church. Christopher would certainly have been one of 'the good fellows amongst us' who 'begin now to be acquainted with a certain parlous book called, as I remember me, *Il Principe* de Nicolo Machiavelli' as Gabriel Harvey wrote to Edmund Spenser the year before Kit Marlowe arrived in Cambridge. Harvey and Spenser were both inclined to Puritanism, though Spenser was later to be close with Raleigh and acquainted with Marlowe, neither of whom had Puritan tendencies. And the heretic Francis Kett, who was at Corpus Christi for some of Kit's time and who was later burned at the stake at Norwich, does not seem to have influenced Marlowe either, as books had the greatest impact for him in his first years at Cambridge. Machiavelli's book quoted by Harvey, *The Prince*, had made its particular contribution to the Renaissance because it described the ruthless attainment of political power. In it the end justified the means. Such a lack of hypocrisy impressed students, though Kit Marlowe by no means wholeheartedly embraced its dicta. In his much misquoted opening speech of *The Jew of Malta* he made ironic criticism of popes:

Machiavelli: Though some speak openly against my books,

> Yet will they read me, and thereby attain
> To Peter's chair . . .

The ensuing lines,

> I count religion but a childish toy,
> And hold there is no sin but ignorance

are part of the speech of such a person, not a statement of Marlowe's own views. These lines should not be taken out of context.

The speech finishes:

> . . . I come not, I
> To read a lecture here in Britain,
> But to present the tragedy of a Jew,
> Who smiles to see how full his bags are cramm'd;
> Which money was not got without my means.

The Jew comes to a bad end, incarcerated in his own cauldron. So are the guilty punished. The play is an ironic morality tale and, in modern terms, a black comedy. In Shakespeare's *The Merchant of Venice* Shylock's words are not regarded as Shakespeare's personal creed; nor should Marlowe be designated as Machiavellian because his character Barabas was.

However, some light is thrown on Kit Marlowe's views by the speech of the French scholar Ramus in *The Massacre at Paris*, before he was murdered, because Marlowe was a scholar and more likely to have identified himself with Ramus.

> Ramus: I knew the Organon to be confus'd
> And I reduc'd it into better form:
> And this for Aristotle will I say,
> That he that despiseth him can ne'er
> Be good in logic or philosophy; . . .

The Duke of Anjou comments, 'Ne'er was there Collier's son so full of pride,' which could be a cry from the heart of the shoemaker's son.

Christopher Marlowe learned of Ramus's work from his lecturer in dialectics, M. Johnes – Kit is noted as one of the Corpus Christi students who were to study under M. Johnes from 29 October 1581. As dialectics was undertaken in the second year, he must have been new to the class then. Three other scholarship holders who entered Corpus Christi in 1580 are grouped with him in the college list. Dialectics dealt with logic, which was less inspiring to a young poet than rhetoric. However, it was important for the clear-thinking mind.

Aristotle and philosophy were studied particularly in the third year, together with dialectics and Christopher's extra-curricular activities included translations of Lucan and Ovid and his writing of *Tamburlaine*. His literal Lucan translations are in blank verse, not in rhymed couplets like his Ovid translations. *Tamburlaine* is also in blank verse, but contains many high-sounding phrases, whereas the Lucan translations stick to the sombre original – though Lucan himself wrote some purple patches.

From the record of the weekly shillings he received for attendance at Corpus, it appears that Christopher was away for part of the fourth term of 1581–2, and he probably went to Canterbury to visit his family then. There are various other absences; one coincided with a similar absence of Thomas Lewgar and probably the two friends spent a holiday together. On an absence in 1585 Kit went to Canterbury, witnessing a will there and leaving his only extant signature. The later 1585–early 1586 accounts are missing, but he was also away during part of 1587, probably making his visit to Rheims.

The Canterbury visit was his first major break from Cambridge, and his return to Corpus was different from the original journey. Arriving as a seasoned student he was greeted by familiarity: the same meagre meals – soup, small pieces of beef, oatmeal – after the Marlowe's welcoming spread; the same church services; the same library, and the green lawns under the open Cambridge sky. And the Marlowe family must have found him different from the inexperienced youth who went away.

In 1583 a play was performed at Corpus Christi and a visitor from Pembroke Hall threw stones. Whether he was a Puritan expressing his faith or a bored member of the audience seeking revenge is not known. Corpus Christi had a gallery in Kit's time on which plays were acted, as did the inn immediately opposite Corpus Christi, and such galleries were incorporated in the stages of the new theatres being built in London. Galleries were to feature in some of the plays, for example in Kit Marlowe's *The Jew of Malta* and Shakespeare's *Romeo and Juliet*. Watching the performance of plays in Cambridge inspired Kit Marlowe's work on *Tamburlaine*.

Did he ever join strolling players, such as the ones who performed at the near-by inn, during his Cambridge years? Unusual absences from Corpus Christi are revealed in the college records in 1584–85 before his visit to Canterbury; he had meals in college while not claiming his residence money, and this is a time when he might have taken to the Cambridgeshire roads with a visiting acting company. There could, of course be several other reasons for the absences – he might by then have met Thomas Walsingham, whose family had Cambridgeshire property, or he could have been involved in his literary activity away from the disturbing early morning bells.

Kit graduated as a Bachelor of Arts on Palm Sunday 1584 and became Dominus Marlyn. He would now have status. In fact, the letter 'D' was already being prefixed to his name in the buttery books before he graduated, so he satisfied the requirements before graduation day.

Supplicating for a Bachelor of Arts degree was complicated. Twelve terms of residence had to be completed. There were two tests in disputation, when the 'respondent' was opposed by three students from other colleges, in Latin, in front of an audience in the public schools. Following this the student was seen by the officials from his own college, before he sat the examinations in the public schools. Having passed these he could supplicate to the Vice-Chancellor to be admitted 'ad respondendum quaestioni'.

Then in the public schools the supplicants were questioned on Aristotle's *Prior Analytics*. Ultimately, on Palm Sunday – the examinations were usually held in the week preceding Ash Wednesday – the successful graduated. Their names were entered in the Grace Book, and Christopher's appears as Marley in the 1583–4 Grace Book.

In 1582 another Thomas destined to be Kit's friend had entered St John's College. This was Thomas Nashe, who was three years younger than Kit. Nashe was to become a pamphleteer almost as well-known as Kit was as a playwright. At Cambridge they worked together on a play called *Dido, Queen of Carthage*, which was taken from Virgil.

Most of the work on *Dido* was done in the later part of 1584 after Kit graduated (could this have some connection with his absences?), in 1585 and in 1586 after Nashe graduated. The play sticks fairly closely to Virgil, and another version of part of it is acted by the players in Shakespeare's *Hamlet*. Nashe later published *Dido, Queen of Carthage* as a joint work by himself and Marlowe, with Marlowe's name in larger letters.

Though Nashe stayed at Cambridge for two years after graduating as a BA, he did not become an MA, as Kit did in 1587. Nashe decided to make literature his living and was preparing a play, *The Anatomie of Absurdite*; but when he took it to London it was not successful. Later, in a pamphlet called *Pierce Peniless*, he wrote bitterly that brainless drudges wax fat while 'the seven liberal sciences and a good leg will scarce get a scholar bread and cheese'. Nashe was to indulge in a pamphlet war with Gabriel Harvey, and to be imprisoned briefly with Ben Jonson in 1597 when their play *The Isle of Dogs* was deemed 'seditious and slanderous matter'.

At some time while he was at Cambridge Kit made the acquaintance of Thomas Walsingham, which was to change his life. Through Thomas, Kit was employed as a government spy, went to London with introductions to literary people, and received patronage. Kit was a house guest of Thomas's at Scadbury in

Chislehurst, sheltering from the plague, at the time of the Dept-ford incident in 1593.

Thomas Walsingham was to succeed to Scadbury after his brother Edmund died in November 1589. Edmund was then thirty-two and Thomas twenty-six. From 1584 onwards, prob-ably just before he met Kit, Thomas had been receiving an annuity of £24 per year under his father's will; had Edmund not died in 1589 and Thomas become the sole heir, this would have grown to £50 after seven years. He thus enjoyed considerable independence.

These Walsinghams were distinguished by their relationship with Sir Francis Walsingham, Queen Elizabeth's Secretary of State and spy chief, whose daughter Frances married Sir Philip Sidney and later the Earl of Essex.

Sir Francis was employing young men to visit Europe in the pre-Armada period to obtain intelligence about the Spanish enemy. King Philip of Spain was the widower of Elizabeth's Catholic half-sister Mary, during whose reign England had been Catholic. Under Elizabeth the Protestantism of their father King Henry VIII returned, though with more dignity than during his time. Philip of Spain was seeking to re-establish Catholicism in England.

Many English Catholics were loyal to Elizabeth but some, with the support of the French, were seeking to make the Catholic Mary Queen of Scots, Elizabeth's cousin (and the mother of the ultimate Protestant successor James), the new ruler of England. As Mary was imprisoned in England and various plots were hatched around her, Sir Francis Walsingham employed spies to watch her and her friends in England and Europe.

His young relative Thomas was a 'recruiting officer', and he enlisted Kit's services for Europe. Whether with his newly ac-quired £24 a year Thomas also patronized Kit's poetry is not clear. (It is possible that the Walsingham family heard of Kit through Nicholas Faunt, a King's School ex-scholar from Kit's time who became attached to Sir Francis's staff.)

Thomas was a year older than Kit and was used to a higher standard of living. Imagine their first meeting, with Thomas attired in embroidered doublet, high ruff and silk breeches, and perhaps with long locks hanging from his head, and Kit in fustian and plain breeches, with short hair! If Thomas were responsible for having the portrait painted it is clear why he had Kit arrayed in richer garments.

What Kit's shoemaker father, or chamber-mate Thomas Lewgar, thought of his grand new acquaintance is interesting speculation. Ambitious Thomas Nashe would be anxious to ally himself with Kit because of his association with Thomas Walsingham.

Kit's European travel did not start immediately, but a friendship was formed with Thomas Walsingham which was to continue for the rest of Kit's life.

The Walsinghams' home was in Kent, the mansion Scadbury, near Chislehurst. As Kit observed it on his way to Canterbury he must have been impressed with his new friend's substance. Kit travelled to Canterbury in 1585, but even if he was known to Thomas by then it is unlikely that he was yet on visiting terms.

During this vacation John Marlowe was able to show off his graduate son. Perhaps this was why Kit was asked to be a signatory to the will of a neighbour, Mistress Katherine Benchkin. All the signatories were connections of the Marlowe family; John Marlowe (who signed as 'Marley'); Christopher; Thomas Arthur, Mistress Marlowe's brother (who may have paid for Kit's early education); and John Moore, husband of Christopher's sister Joan. John Moore was a shoemaker like John Marlowe, and had married Joan when she was thirteen. The will is now in the archives of the Maidstone County Records Office. It is interesting to see John Marlowe's signature in a neat, clear hand; he was not uneducated, for all his bluster.

St Ben't's churchyard adjoins Corpus Christi, which had once been known as St Ben't's college; and the church, churchyard and Corpus Christi Old Court, which overlooks them, can be seen today, across the road from the public house (now called the Eagle) with its fine playactors' gallery. This may have been the rendezvous for meetings between Thomas Walsingham and Kit, as once Kit became a graduate he could visit it with more freedom.

Before Kit graduated in his second degree and became an MA, he was to have experience as a government agent. He was also to decide, as Thomas Nashe did, to make literature his career. But he did not emulate Nashe by abandoning his MA, and fought tenaciously for the right to acquire it. He *was* to abandon plans for becoming a clergyman. His friend Thomas Lewgar became a clergyman and he and Kit saw little of each other after Cambridge.

Kit's Rheims trip and its implications deserve a separate chapter. In the 1587 Corpus Christi Grace Book, Kit Marlowe's MA was recorded. To have gained this second degree, to have written two plays and a number of translations and to have travelled to Rheims as a government agent shows remarkable stamina. It was becoming clear how he achieved so much in his short life.

Also, a stimulant to his work on *Tamburlaine* had appeared. In 1586 an account of Tamburlaine and his conquests appeared in George Whetstone's *Mirror*, and this must have strengthened Kit's intention to take his dramatized version to London.

3 · Rheims

In 1586 the Babington plot to assassinate Queen Elizabeth and put Mary Queen of Scots on the English throne was frustrated by Sir Francis Walsingham. Babington had been a page to the Earl of Shrewsbury, 'keeper' of the imprisoned ex-Queen of Scots, and had developed a passion for Mary. He became involved with Mary's supporters in Paris and carried letters to her in England. Philip of Spain agreed to assist Mary's champions to ensure the return of Catholicism to England, and a priest, John Ballard, joined Babington. They planned an uprising to dispense with Elizabeth and her ministers and enthrone Mary.

Sir Francis Walsingham introduced a special agent. This was the infamous Robert Poley, who was to be present at the Deptford incident in 1593. Poley gained the confidence of the conspirators and collected incriminating evidence, which he gave to Sir Francis. Then Ballard was arrested. Under torture he revealed further details of the plot. Others were imprisoned.

Until this time Elizabeth had not believed that her cousin was personally involved in this scheming surrounding her. There was ample evidence of Mary's complicity in the Babington plot. The leading conspirators were condemned to death for high treason, and Mary, whether she was a willing or unwitting party to the plot, was eventually beheaded.

Elizabeth had doubts even then. Nevertheless she agreed that the desire of European Catholics to remove her from the English throne, of which Sir Francis had warned her ever since he had been ambassador in Paris, really existed.

She began treating seriously information Sir Francis's agents collected about the Armada being prepared in Spain. Sea-captain

Francis Drake delayed the Armada when he 'singed the King of Spain's beard', and attacked the fleet as it lay in Cadiz harbour; but the Prince of Parma's troops were already gathering in the Low Countries waiting to join with the Armada for the attack on England.

At this highly charged time some divinity students from Cambridge, particularly from Caius College where Ballard of the Babington plot had studied, were absconding to France before taking their MAS. They were going to a seminary at Rheims run by a Dr Allen, which was a haven for dissident English Catholics. This seminary had opened in Douai in 1568 under Dr Richard Smith and during ten peaceful years scholars like Edward Campion and a man who was to be Kit's friend, Thomas Watson, studied there. Then in 1579 it moved to Rheims and became a centre for English disaffection, though some scholars still pursued serious studies. As Kit Marlowe wrote in *The Massacre at Paris* (Act v, Scene ii),

> Henry: Did he not draw a sort of English priests
> From Douai to the seminary at Rheims,
> To hatch forth treason 'gainst their natural queen?
> Did he not cause the king of Spain's huge fleet
> To threaten England and to menace me?

Kit was himself sent by the Walsinghams to the Rheims seminary in late 1586 or early 1587 to pretend he was a potential convert and to report on its activities to Sir Francis Walsingham.

It was Kit's first journey outside England; Canterbury was near the Kentish coast, but this time he was to cross the Channel to France. He probably made the journey with a group of absconding divinity students, and Thomas Walsingham may have accompanied him till he linked up with this party.

To a Lucan translator of Kit's imagination the Channel would be 'the Rubicon', and crossing it a decision as weighty as Caesar's. He was fitted for such a mission not only by temperament, but because he had sufficient knowledge of the French language from

Canterbury Huguenots to understand, and make himself understood, in France.

After landing in Calais, horses were available for them. Their route was through villages and countryside to Paris, and from there to Rheims.

Paris was in many ways like a larger Canterbury. One feature of equal importance in both cities was the cathedral. But Paris's Notre Dame stood on an island in the River Seine, while Canterbury's was on a hill near the narrower Stour; and Canterbury's King's School and ecclesiastical buildings were fewer than the many educational and religious institutions of Paris, which included the Sorbonne University. Nevertheless, the mixture of cloister and market enclosed by walls was common to both. One aspect of Paris which was absent from Canterbury was the influence of classicism in the new architecture. Pillars, statues and ornamentation adorned some of the richer Parisian houses, while Canterbury was still relatively medieval in appearance.

Kit would wish he could explore Paris, and visit the Sorbonne and some colleges, instead of being hurried on to Rheims. In *The Massacre at Paris* (Act I, scene ii) the Guise says:

> Paris has full five hundred colleges,
> As monasteries, priories, abbeys, and halls,
> Wherein are thirty thousand able men,
> Besides a thousand sturdy student Catholics;
> And more, – of my knowledge, in one cloister keeps
> Five hundred fat Franciscan friars and priests.

There was a beautiful and richly ornamented building to be seen at Rheims – the cathedral. But neither Renaissance nor Reformation had made much impression on the Rheims seminary. Here abstinence and strict self-discipline prevailed.

Kit must have been horrified to find that fasting was compulsory for two days in each week. And though all the seminary's students were not Catholics – as in the case of Thomas Watson at Douai –

there would be Catholic services to attend by an alleged prospective convert. As Kit usually found Church of England services long, while he was demonstrating his patriotism by making this spy journey, the high Catholic ceremony would be very irksome. The façade of the Rheims seminary, which is still standing, is austere. When Kit emerged, having mendaciously promised to spread disaffection in England, perhaps he gave thanks to Ceres, the classical goddess of the crops of the surrounding farms, for his deliverance.

The return journey would be enjoyable. He had been a long way from the shoemaker's shop and was becoming a man of the world. The spy trip was important for his development because it added a dimension to his experience which he could not have gained in Canterbury, Cambridge or London.

Back at Cambridge he was to receive a nasty shock. On 31 March, Christopher, Thomas Lewgar and five others from Corpus Christi had been 'granted grace' to supplicate for their Master of Arts degrees. But Christopher's grace was withdrawn. Information about his visit to Rheims had reached the authorities. Not only had he been absent from Corpus Christi, but his loyalty to Protestantism was in doubt.

Should Christopher forego his second degree or should he appeal to the powers that had sent him on this mission to clear his name with the university? He chose the second course. What follows throws light on Sir Francis Walsingham's way of working as well as on the forces shaping Kit's career.

Sir Francis attended the Privy Council on the day before the letter to the university authorities was drawn up. So he was not a signatory to the document the Council dispatched – 'cover' for the spy chief for this centre of absconding divinity students? The document was signed by Archbishop Whitgift, Sir Christopher Hatton (Lord Chancellor), Lord Hunsdon (Lord Chamberlain), Lord Burleigh (Lord Treasurer) and Sir James Crofts (Comptroller.) It is in the *Privy Council Registers*, Elizabeth, vi, 381 b. In his book *The Death of Christopher Marlowe* (1925) Dr Hotson established that the 'Christopher Morley' specified in this 1587 document was Kit Marlowe. The document read:

Whereas it was reported that Christofer Morley was determined to haue gone beyond the seas to Reames and there to remaine, Their Lordships thought good to certefie that he had no such intent, but that in all his accions he had beaued him selfe orderlie and discreetlie wherebie he had done her Majestie good service, & deserued to be rewarded for his faithfull dealinge: Their Lordships request was that the rumor thereof should be allaied by all possible meanes, and that he should be furthered in the degree he was to take this next Commencement: Because it was not her Majesties pleasure that anie one emploied as he had been in matters touching the benefit of his Countrie should be defamed by those that are ignorant in th' affaires he went about.

The Master of Corpus when Kit's MA was in jeopardy was Dr Norgate. On his death during the same year, Dr Copcott, previously Vice-Chancellor of the university and an appointee of Lord Burleigh, succeeded Dr Norgate. It has been suggested that the portrait thought to be of Kit might have been presented to Dr Copcott in gratitude for his intervention in the granting of Kit's MA. Whether the benefactor was Dr Copcott (who may thus have been repaid by Kit's friends) or Dr Norgate, or both in awe of the Privy Council document, or neither, he duly graduated in 1587 and left Cambridge with two degrees.

The fact that he fought to receive his MA, a degree sought after by divinity students, even though he had decided not to take Holy Orders, gives some idea of his respect for learning and divinity. When hearsay stories of his wild utterances are recounted it is wise to remember this.

Christopher made the journey from Cambridge to London in the late spring of 1587. He was twenty-three years old. He had completed *Tamburlaine*, Part One, and had made notes for Part Two. With Nashe he had worked on *Dido, Queen of Carthage* from Virgil, and alone he had translated poetry by Ovid and Lucan. He had graduated as BA and MA, and in Her Majesty's service he had been to Rheims, this latter being acknowledged by the great Privy Council itself. Kit's journey from Canterbury had been undertaken in the winter, and his new move was in the season of high promise – late spring. Green trees, blossom and perhaps sunshine and blue skies attended him. By agreeing to work for Sir Francis Walsingham he had gained the powerful friendship of Thomas Walsingham, who may already have patronized his poetry. Introductions to literary circles would come more easily for him than for Shakespeare and Nashe.

But even now his enormous success and untimely disappearance could not have been forecast. The university authorities, though he had been supported by the Privy Council, had not placed his name top of the graduation list. The Privy Council document had been earned by his Rheims visit – he had not received an unsolicited gift from high places. Yet he was fortunate to be in a position where Privy Council recognition was necessary – and he had gained helpful supplementary money for his literary career from his spy travels.

If Kit Marlowe had not been born in Canterbury he would not have attended King's School, he may not have received a scholarship to Cambridge University, and without an abrasive father like John Marlowe he might have lacked the courage to be a spy. Circumstance was on his side. It was to contribute further to his rise – when he was to become the leading playwright of the new London theatre.

4 · Tamburlaine in London

The London to which Kit Marlowe went was too big for its walls. Many houses were outside the city proper and their inhabitants came in through 'gates' to the city. Some of the names survive in street and tube station titles such as Aldgate, Moorgate and Bishopsgate.

There were several theatres when Kit arrived in London in 1587. Two in the northern area beyond Bishopsgate were the Theatre and the Curtain. James Burbage, of the famous theatrical family, had constructed the Theatre in 1576 and its timbers were later rebuilt into the Globe in 1598. As the city authorities were not well disposed towards the stage and Puritans supported this opposition, it was safer for the theatres to be outside the city walls. Acting companies could also perform in inn yards inside the walls, where galleries above central square areas were common, but as these did not make for artistic production and allowed for changing of lines, they were not the stages the playwrights favoured for their works. The arrival of the great dramatists brought a need for theatres specifically constructed for their plays; and the status given to actors by patronage also made these buildings necessary.

An acting company became 'legal' if it was 'patronized' by a nobleman – an Act passed in 1572 stated that a company could not perform in public unless under the name of a baron or someone higher in the peerage. Until this time strolling companies had been motley collections, sometimes more like circuses than serious actors, containing acrobats, bearwards, minstrels, fortune-tellers, and other fairground characters as well as players. Under the 1572 Act of Parliament a patronized acting company received a licence

28

to perform. Elizabeth herself allowed a troupe to exist called the Queen's Men, and her successor James I was to take over the Lord Chamberlain's Men, who became the King's Men.

One of the first noblemen to give his name to a company was Elizabeth's favourite, the Earl of Leicester. In 1574 Letters Patent gave the Queen's permission to members of Leicester's Men, including James Burbage, to 'use, exercise and occupy the art and faculty of playing comedies, tragedies, stage plays ... for the recreation of our loving subjects and our solace and pleasure'. The players performed at the Earl's country mansion at Kenilworth before the Queen in 1575. Then in 1576 James Burbage built the Theatre in Shoreditch, beyond Bishopsgate, for Leicester's Men to occupy. Other companies performed there later, and the Burbage family ultimately went on to different associations. But Robert Dudley, Earl of Leicester, played an important part in establishing the respectability of the theatre against Puritan and civic hostility.

An actor important to Kit Marlowe was Edward Alleyn, first heard of as a youth in Worcester's Men. He was soon to join the troupe of Lord Howard, the Lord Admiral. Lord Howard of Effingham, the Queen's cousin, was to be England's admiral in the successful defence against the Armada, and his players performed at court at Christmas 1585. He himself was important politically as well as through his relationship to the Queen. His was the troupe for whom Kit Marlowe was to write most of his plays.

A company Kit later worked for was Lord Pembroke's. This troupe, while making a large contribution to the development of historical drama, was to have difficult times, demonstrating that noblemen sometimes gave only their names to companies. When Pembroke's Men were driven out of London by the plague in 1593 and went bankrupt on tour, the Earl did not rescue them with a subsidy. Henslowe wrote in a letter to Edward Alleyn that Pembroke's Men could not 'save their charges with travel on the road' and had to pawn their costumes to stay alive. By this time

Marlowe and Shakespeare, who had both worked on historical plays for Pembroke's Men, had moved – Marlowe back to Edward Alleyn for *Doctor Faustus*, and Shakespeare to the Lord Chamberlain's Men. There was in fact much movement between groups, and sometimes whole troupes merged, as when the Admiral's Men joined with Lord Strange's in 1587, and both later joined the Chamberlain's Men.

When Kit arrived in London in 1587 the person to whom he had an introduction was Thomas Watson, the poet, Latin scholar, madrigal writer and general man-about-town. Tom Watson had been acquainted with the Walsingham family since he met Sir Francis during his ambassadorship in Paris. Watson was to become Kit's mentor in London. The Walsinghams were patrons of poetry rather than the theatre, but Tom Watson, who was a convivial fellow, knew actors. He was residing at Bishopsgate, working as tutor to William Cornwallis's son in 1587, and may have initiated Kit into the theatre immediately after his arrival.

Tom Watson was seven years older than Kit. He had travelled in Europe, studying at the seminary at Douai and in one of the Roman law schools in Italy. He suffered from having too many talents; they diversified his interests, and his frothy sense of humour inclined him to indiscipline in their management. Watson's contemporaries ranked him as a poet with Spenser and Sidney, but few of his works survive. He published a book of madrigals in 1590 with William Byrd; Byrd is still famous but Watson is not. William Cornwallis, to whose son Watson was tutor, said that writing plays was Watson's daily occupation, but none are known to survive. Watson may have been accident prone. Certainly he suffered more than Kit in the three-way sword fight between himself, Marlowe and Bradley which was to take place in 1589.

The Cornwallis family, by whom Watson was employed in 1587, was musical and cultivated, but though Watson had the patronage of the great Walsinghams he did not aspire to marriage with the Cornwallis family, and married the sister of another retainer, Swift. Swift, however, wanted to marry a Cornwallis lady, and after Watson died in 1592 the Cornwallis family claimed that *he*, Watson, had composed Swift's love-letters, and that he could 'devise twenty fictions and knaveries in a play, which was his daily practice and his living'.

One of Watson's 'pranks' was to encourage a woman of the parish of St Helen, Bishopsgate, to believe that she was the illegitimate child of King Philip of Spain, from the time when Philip had been in England. She thought the marks on her back resembled the royal arms. Watson suggested that these marks could grow greater and that she would even have a lock of hair like gold wire in her head. Some of the jokes in Marlowe's *The Jew of Malta* seem to have had their origin in Watson's particular sense of humour.

People who suggest that the three-way sword fight in Shakespeare's *Romeo and Juliet* is based on Watson, Marlowe and Bradley, make the mistake of casting Kit Marlowe, not Watson, as Mercutio, thus disregarding Watson's personality and age – he was not at all like Romeo. It does seem that the character of Mercutio may have been based on Watson – he had the same jesting facility with words, which the acute Shakespeare would have noticed.

A piece of ill luck had befallen Watson in 1585 when another poet, Abraham Fraunce, translated Watson's Latin verse 'Amyntas' into English, claiming it as his own work and dedicating it to Lady Mary Sidney. Kit Marlowe made certain no such fate befell Watson's last Latin poem, 'Amyntae Gaudia', which he personally published in his dead friend's name in 1592, and dedicated to the same lady, Mary Sidney, Countess of Pembroke. Watson's verse was, however, lacking in inspiration. For example:

This latter night amidst my troubled rest
A dismal dream my fearful heart appalled,
Whereof the sum was this; Love made a feast

To which all neighbour saints and gods were called;
 The cheer was more than mortal men can think
 And mirth grew on, by taking in their drink ...

And thou, Oh Death! When I possess my heart,
Dispatch me then at once, Why so?
By promise thou are bound to end my smart.
Why, if thy heart return, then what's thy woe?
 That, brought from cold, it never will desire
 To rest with me, which am more hot than fire.

(Hekatompathia, 1582)

Tom Watson said of himself in his dedication to the Earl of Arundel of *Sophoclis Antigone* in 1581:

> While I altogether devoted my early days to study, and while far from my native land, I passed a lustrum and a half, learning to utter words of diverse sounds ... So far as I was able I paid worship to the Muses, wherever I went. Justinian, too, was especially dear. But Mars often broke in upon reluctant Pallas ...

This was to be true not only of battles interrupting his earlier life, but of the Bradley sword fight which was to become the tragedy of his life, though touching Kit Marlowe less devastatingly.

This was the man who introduced Kit Marlowe to theatrical London.

London itself, outside whose walls the theatres were beginning to appear, was a crowded city with cobbled streets and the Thames as busy thoroughfares. Boats hurried up and down the river with ferrymen shouting 'Eastward Ho' and 'Westward Ho'. A typical remark came from Frederick, Duke of Württemburg, in 1592; 'It is a very populous city, so that one can scarcely pass along the streets, because of the throng' (W. B. Rye, *England as seen by Foreigners*, 1865).

There was a bridge over the river with shops on both sides,

some of them bookshops. St Paul's churchyard was a centre for printers, and a meeting place for the literary community who had no compunction about pasting posters and pamphlets on handy pillars. The spire of St Paul's, which had been hit by lightning in 1562, had a flat tower; and windmills stood in the fields just outside the walls. There was anti-foreign feeling among many of the inhabitants, not only against the Spanish but against Flemish merchants who took work from native-born Londoners. The equivalent of 'Go Home Dutchman' was found written more than once on the sides of Calvinistic churches. London was a metropolis for trade as well as for the arts, and Kit Marlowe, who had briefly seen Paris, must nevertheless have found London daunting. The company of older, seasoned Tom Watson would have been comforting.

There is no definite proof that the first performance of *Tamburlaine* starred Edward Alleyn, though the play was staged by the Admiral's Men and Alleyn was to be famous in the part. No one has established when Alleyn joined the Admiral's Men or when they allowed such a young actor (he was two years Kit's junior) to become their leading player. But it is probable that the new young playwright and the aspiring young actor began together. *Tamburlaine* needed a charismatic actor – a shepherd conquering the world must be dominating – and Ned Alleyn was the most magnetic actor of the late Elizabethan period.

Though Thomas Kyd's *The Spanish Tragedy*, the other major play of the early days of the theatre, was to be successful and influential, it did not have the impact of *Tamburlaine*. The combination of Marlowe's poetry and Alleyn's performance was to make *Tamburlaine* a catalyst. When Kit Marlowe read about Tamburlaine in the Master's library at King's School, a train of events was set in motion resulting in English drama as it is still known. Kit Marlowe was to write other plays, Shakespeare and Jonson were to follow, more actors were to dominate the boards. But the coming together of Kit Marlowe, Ned Alleyn and the new theatres with *Tamburlaine* was a definitive inspiration. It is fitting that the twenty-three-year-old 'father' of drama should have been born in the spiritual capital, Canterbury, and educated on scholarships. Drama belongs to the people and Kit Marlowe was one of the people. Shakespeare was to have Marlowe's example to follow; Marlowe's good fortune was to have gained the right introductions and to find a suitable actor for his plays – at the time when theatres were being built.

Much unfounded legend has grown up round Kit Marlowe's life. Hearsay material exists from unhappy playwrights like Greene and Kyd; and the informer Baines said much in support of Kyd. A few fellow-travellers went along with Kyd and Baines. But there were favourable comments from friends, like Ned Blout the publisher and playwright John Marston, and Shakespeare himself quoted more from Marlowe than from any other playwright. Further damage has been done to Kit's reputation recently by alarmed Shakespeare purists, because of the suggestion that Shakespeare did not exist and that the plays were written by Kit Marlowe, incognito. Marlowe is denigrated for this, though he is in no way responsible for what is alleged about him four hundred years later!

When it is stated that Shakespeare's plays are better constructed than Marlowe's it should be remembered that Marlowe came first. Shakespeare improved on Marlowe's already demonstrated technique. Marlowe gave life to the dramatic form which Shakespeare used. Marlowe and Shakespeare were involved with Pembroke's Men at the same time, and with several other playwrights including Kyd and Greene. Some works later revised by Shakespeare, and attributed to him, began with Marlowe and Kyd. After Marlowe and Kyd died Shakespeare came into his own, until he was ultimately succeeded by Beaumont and Fletcher. But in 1587, when *Tamburlaine* was staged, the leading playwrights were Marlowe because of *Tamburlaine*, and Kyd because of *The Spanish Tragedy*. That *Tamburlaine* was an instant success was proved by the staging of *Tamburlaine*, Part Two, within several months of Part One's first performance.

The play audiences who saw *Tamburlaine* were a cross-section of London dwellers, with the exception of Puritans and workers employed in the afternoons. Plays were staged in the afternoons because there was no artificial light for evening productions. Rehearsals could be conducted at night by candlelight, and in the morning.

Thomas Nashe, in his defence of drama against 'shallow-brained censurers', claimed that it kept gentlemen from harmful pursuits.

For whereas the afternoon being the idlest time of the day, wherein men who are their own masters (as Gentlemen of the Court, the Inns of Court, and the number of Captains and Soldiers about London) do wholly bestow themselves upon pleasure and that pleasure they divide (how virtuously it skills not) either into gaming, following of harlots, drinking, or seeing a play, is it not better (since of four extremes all the world cannot keep them but they will choose one) they should betake them to the least, which is plays?

Often women accompanied these gentlemen, a fact that Nashe does not mention.

The poor were also represented. Crosse, the author of *Vertue's Common-wealth*, wrote in 1603: 'pinched, needy creatures, that live of almes, with scarce clothes for their backs or food for their bellies, make hard shift that they will see a play ...'

The poet Sir John Davies wrote of one stage-struck fellow:

> ... First, he doth rise at ten; and at eleven
> He goes to Gyls, where he doth eate till one;
> Then sees a Play till sixe, and sups at seven;
> And after supper, straight to bed is gone;
> And there till ten next day he doth remaine,
> And then he dines, and sees a Comedy
> And then he suppes, and goes to bed againe.

Not all plays lasted till six. The Prologue of Shakespeare's *Romeo and Juliet* mentions 'the two hours' traffic of our stage', and plays usually started at two or two-thirty.

Another section of the audience was the groundlings or 'penny-knaves' who occupied the standing room close to and around the stage. This was made up of soldiers and sailors on leave, artisans on holiday and groups of workers on public holidays. The groundlings had more full-blooded tastes than discriminatory onlookers, and Kit Marlowe probably despaired when they showed greater appreciation of a bloodthirsty murder than of beautiful poetry. Some playwrights, like Kyd and later Webster, did little to temper blood with poetry, while Marlowe and even Shakespeare did not omit violence. *The Massacre at Paris*, the most 'corrupt' of Marlowe's texts, has kept the murders and appears to have had the poetry cut. Such was crowd-pleasing editing.

The early theatres were open-roofed and while Elizabethan audiences seem to have been hardy, playwrights could blame bad weather for small houses. Webster complained in 1612 that *The White Devil* had small audiences because it was 'in so dull a time of winter and in so open and black a theatre'.

Kit Marlowe's plays were the best attended of his time. For example, in February 1592 at the Rose Theatre, Henslowe's list of takings shows *The Jew of Malta* as easily the most popular.

Feb. 19	Fryer Bacune	17s 3d
21	Mulomurco	29s
22	Orlando	16s 6d
23	Spanes comodye Donne Oracoe	13s 6d
24	Sir John Mandevell	12s 6d
25	Harey of Cornwell	32s
26	the Jewe of Malltuse	50s

The Massacre at Paris (known as *The Guise*), *The Jew of Malta*, both *Tamburlaines*, and *Harey the VI* (at least partially written by Marlowe) always drew large audiences, and though Henslowe's records do not go back to 1587, *Tamburlaine*'s initial success can be judged by the quick staging of the sequel.

Although scenery was not used in the early theatres except for the judicious placing of balconies, curtains and properties, attention was paid to costumes. Edward Alleyn was fond of fine garments and the majesty of *Tamburlaine* was as much to his liking as to the audience's. Entries for productions of *Tamburlaine* in Henslowe's Diary in the early 1590s show expensive materials, and especially copper-lace, being purchased for him.

In 1587 plays were still staged in innyards as well as in the new theatres, and there were over fifty inns in London, the larger ones often having regular performances of plays. Belle Savage's Inn on Ludgate Hill, the Bull in Bishopsgate Street, and the Bell and the Crosskeys in Gracechurch Street, were examples. These stagings, like the theatre performances, usually began at two in the afternoon, finishing in time for spectators to get home before dark. Decorated signs outside inns, like plays, were meant to attract customers.

When an Elizabethan theatre was about to begin a performance a flag was raised on the roof, a trumpet was blown and a drum sounded. For lesser stagings in inn yards, as well as for theatre performances, bills were posted. Alehouses, eating places and Inns of Court were likely centres from which to attract audiences. A company on tour would parade through a country town like a circus. Kit Marlowe would have seen such parades in Cambridge and must have approved the better organization of the London theatres.

In 1587 Watson, Nashe, Peele, Greene and Kyd were already in London and Kit Marlowe had arrived in mid-year. Of the poets, Raleigh was a favourite at court, Sir Philip Sidney had died the year before, Spenser was still in Ireland and Donne (whose daughter was to be Ned Alleyn's second wife) was not yet known. (Alleyn's first wife was Henslowe's daughter.) Shakespeare was not yet in London, though his friend from Stratford, Richard Field, who had apprenticed himself in London to the Huguenot printer Thomas Vautrollier, married Vautrollier's widow and took over the press in 1587. Field was to publish Shakespeare's partner poem for Marlowe's *Hero and Leander*, *Venus and Adonis* in 1593.

The fame of the Kit Marlowe–Ned Alleyn partnership is borne out in the 1633 Quarto edition of *The Jew of Malta*, the earliest surviving text of this play. They are referred to in an Epistle and a Prologue, both added by Thomas Heywood. The Epistle (to Master Thomas Hammon, of Gray's Inn, etc.) begins:

This play, composed by so worthy an author as Master Marlowe, and the part of the Jew presented by so unimitable an actor as Master Alleyn.

And the Prologue to the Stage (at The Cockpit):

> We know not how our play may pass this stage,
> But by the best of poets in that age
> The Malta-Jew had being and was made;
> And he then by the best of actors play'd:
> In Hero and Leander one did gain
> A lasting memory; In Tamburlaine,
> This Jew, with others many, th'other wan
> The attribute of peerless, being a man
> Whom we may rank with (doing no one wrong)
> Proteus for shapes, and Roscius for a tongue . . .

Roscius was a famous Roman actor.

Thomas Nashe was even more complimentary to Alleyn in 1592 when he wrote in *Pierce Penilesse*: 'Not Roscius, not Esope, those tragedians admyred before Christ was borne, could ever performe more in action than famous Ned Allen . . .'

To what extent Kit Marlowe changed the text of *Tamburlaine* after he arrived in London is not clear. But as extra lines, and even extra actions, had been interpolated by others into pre-1590 performances of the *Tamburlaines*, the publisher Richard Jones, in dedicating the printed text in 1590, outlined what must have been heartfelt by Kit Marlowe.

I have purposely omitted and left out some fond and frivolous gestures, digressing and, in my poor opinion, far unmeet for the matter, which I thought might seem more tedious unto the wise than any way else to be regarded, though haply they have been of some vain, conceited fondlings greatly gaped at, what times they were showed upon the stage in their graced deformities. Nevertheless, now to be mixtured in print with such matter of worth, it would prove a great disgrace to so honourable and stately a history.

The title page of Richard Jones's 1590 first edition made clear that the *Tamburlaines* had been performed in inn yards, as it read 'two tragical discourses, as they were sundry times showed upon stages in the City of London'.

It is likely that Tom Watson took Kit to some performances when he arrived in London, where he observed the need for martial speeches and many murders to excite the crowd. Though he may already have visited London from Cambridge, he would not have viewed the audiences then with professional eyes. Residence in London near the theatres, and the company of a person like Tom Watson, would give him confidence to aim for success, as King's School had given him the confidence to gain a scholarship to Cambridge University.

Tamburlaine's opening speech begins:

> Mycetes: Brother Cosroe, I find myself agriev'd;
> Yet insufficient to express the same,
> For it requires a great and thundering speech.

There are many 'great and thundering' speeches in *Tamburlaine*. To have caught the mood of pre-Armada London so speedily shows quick initiation into the theatre as well as quick-wittedness and good luck.

There is no record of bitterness or rivalry on Tom Watson's part after his young friend's success. As in the sword fight, when he was to rescue Kit, he was generous. Other playwrights like Greene, and Kit's erstwhile friend Nashe, were not so kind. Marlowe had written in the Prologue to *Tamburlaine*:

> From jigging veins of rhyming mother wits

> And such conceits as clownage keeps in pay
> We'll lead you to the stately tent of war . . .

and Nashe wrote in his preface to Greene's *Menaphon* (1589):

> Idiot art-masters that intrude themselves to our ears as the alcumists
> of eloquence, who (mounted on the stage of arrogance) think to
> outbrave better pens with the swelling bombast of bragging blank
> verse.

Nashe later claimed he never abused Marlowe, and that is true
of his activities after Kit's death. He published their jointly written play from their Cambridge days, *Dido, Queen of Carthage*,
prefacing it with a Latin elegy to Kit's memory; and in his Preface
to *Christs Tears over Jerusalem* (1594) he referred to 'poor deceased Marlowe'. He also, in *Lenten Stuffe* (1599), wrote a parody
of Marlowe's unfinished poem *Hero and Leander*.

Greene was vitriolic, referring in *Perimedes the Black-Smith*
(1588) to '. . . daring God out of heauen with that Atheist
Tamburlan . . . such mad and scoffing poets, that have propheticall
spirits, as bred of Merlins race . . .'

'Daring God out of heaven with that atheist Tamburlaine'
is taken out of context, as is Machiavelli's speech in the opening
of *The Jew of Malta*, to 'prove' Marlowe's lack of belief. The
actual scene, in *Tamburlaine*, Part Two (Act v), depicts Tamburlaine trying to defy death as he had defied everything else, and
not succeeding. He initially says:

> Now, Mahomet, if thou have any power,
> Come down thyself, and work a miracle . . .

After nothing happens, he adds:

> Well, soldiers, Mahomet remains in hell;
> He cannot hear the voice of Tamburlaine.
> Seek out another godhead to adore:
> The God that sits in heaven, if any god,
> For he is God alone, and none but he.

> . . . Whatsoe'er it be,
> Sickness or death can never conquer me.

But, soon after, he admits:

> See, where my slave, the ugly monster Death,
> Shaking and quivering, pale and wan for fear,
> Stands aiming at me with his murdering dart,
> Who flies away at every glance I give,
> And, when I look away, comes stealing on.

Tamburlaine loses his last battle, and dies. Mahomet, who was 'dared out of heaven' (not God), is avenged. Right ultimately wins.

Marlowe has suffered much from misquotation and misrepresentation.

Greene added, in *Farewell to Folly*, that Marlowe, the 'Cobblers eldest son', was a 'propheticall full mouth' and that a pedlar was 'fain to bargain for the life of Tamburlaine to wrap up his sweet powders in those unsavory papers'. Greene was an unhappy soul, and came to a sad end in poverty.

In the summer of 1587 no such clouds were on the horizon. *Tamburlaine*, Part One, had been staged by the Admiral's Men with such success that Kit had prepared a sequel, and the notes he had brought from Cambridge were put to good use. In Part Two Tamburlaine continued his conquests, though both Zenocrate and Tamburlaine were dead by the end of the play. (Had Kit exhausted the material, or did the triumph of right demand these deaths?)

As 1587 was the year before the Spanish Armada, martial verse was at the height of its appeal – a zenith which continued in the wake of England's victory. This patriotism was mainly responsible for the success of rousing plays, and as *Tamburlaine* was the leader of the fashion, it was to be copied by aspiring playwrights.

George Peele's *The Battle of Alcazar* was one example. Another was *Alphonsus, King of Aragon*, by Robert Greene, who later referred to *Tamburlaine* as 'unsavory papers'. George Peele was to speak kindly of Marlowe (and Watson) in 1593 in his poem 'The Honour of the Garter', dedicated to his patron the Earl of Northumberland, who had been made a Knight of the Garter.

> Watson, worthy many Epitaphes
> For his sweet Poesie, for Amintas teares
> And joyes so well set downe. And after thee
> Why hie thee not, unhappy in thine end,
> Marley, the Muses darling, for thy verse,
> Fitte to write passions for the soules below.

In *Tamburlaine*, Part One, there is a cruel scene where the conquered Emperor of the Turks, Bajazeth, is carried on stage in a cage and then brought out to be Tamburlaine's footstool. Later Bajazeth and his wife Zabina kill themselves on the side of the cage. In a ruthless age this was great theatre. Zenocrate was allowed to feel pity and remorse, but eventually married an unrepentant Tamburlaine at the end of Part One.

Another exciting ingredient was the new geography. News of voyages to distant lands and discoveries of countries previously unknown had permeated to London, Cambridge and Canterbury. That Kit Marlowe was inspired by the elastic horizons of the known world is clear from *Tamburlaine*. Of scholarly bent, he related them to Ortelius's atlas, even reproducing the atlas's mistakes.

In *Tamburlaine*, Part Two, Kit Marlowe wrote a line which was quoted and misquoted more than any other of the period. It was 'Holla, ye pamper'd jades of Asia', which Tamburlaine shouted as he entered with his chariot drawn by kings instead of horses. Even Shakespeare used it:

> Pistol: . . . Shall pack-horses
> And hollow pampered jades of Asia,
> Which cannot go but thirty miles a day,
> Compare with Caesars and with Canibals?
>
> (*Henry IV*, Part Two)

and Beaumont and Fletcher:

> . . . Wee-hee,
> My pampered jade of Asia.

Ben Jonson was to refer to 'Tamberlanes and Tamer-Chams' some years later, and it is further evidence of *Tamburlaine*'s impact that its quotations and misquotations echoed for so long.

When the *Tamburlaines* were printed in 1590 some additions were included which could not have been in the original perform- ances. These were 'cross-references' with Spenser's long poem *The Faerie Queen* and information from *The Practice of Fortifica- tion* by Paul Ive, printed in 1589. More will be said about Spenser, whom Walter Raleigh brought from Ireland. Paul Ive was a Kentishman who had also attended Corpus Christi. He was known to both the Walsingham and Raleigh circles, and had been em- ployed by Sir Richard Grenville to construct coastal defences in Cornwall during Raleigh's Lord Lieutenancy. Though Kit may have read the book in manuscript (as he could also have done with *The Faerie Queen*) it could not have been available in 1587. When he was preparing the plays for printing in 1590 he took this opportunity of bringing them up to date.

In 1587, having had two great successes in a matter of months, Kit Marlowe was like Tamburlaine:

> Over my zenith hang a blazing star
> That may endure till heaven be dissolv'd . . .

But tragedy was to strike in a performance by the Admiral's Men of *Tamburlaine*, Part Two, which was to strengthen the opposition of Puritans to the theatre and temporarily halt all performances.

Philip Gawdy, in a letter of November 1587, described what happened:

The Lord Admiral's Men and players having a device in their play to tie one of their fellows to a post and so shoot him to death, having borrowed their calivers, one of the player's hands swerved his piece being charged with bullet, missed the fellow he aimed at and killed a child and a woman great with child forthwith, and hurt another man in the head very sore.

The scene in Act V of *Tamburlaine*, Part Two, has the Governor of Babylon tied on to the wall.

Amyras: See, now, my lord, how brave the captain hangs!
Tamburlaine: 'Tis brave indeed, my boy; well done!
                      Shoot first, my lord, and then the rest shall follow.
Theridamas: Then have at him, to begin withal.
     (Theridamas shoots at the Governor)

After that the accident occurred; whether Theridamas or one of the 'rest' that followed had the loaded gun is not known, and, if in a less warlike time such a tragedy could have happened at all bears reflection. The same atmosphere that helped the play's success also contributed to the tragedy in its staging.

In Part Two, Tamburlaine said:

> There is a God, full of revenging wrath,
> From whom the thunder and the lightning breaks,
> *Whose scourge I am*, and him I will obey.

In understanding the killings and in correcting Greene's misinterpretation of 'daring God out of heaven', two aspects need to be considered: one is Marlowe's irony, which is also overlooked in *The Jew of Malta*, and the other is the serious idea of the pagan tyrant as 'the scourge of God'.

The 'scourge of God' theory has cropped up at various times; great wars have been God's scourge, and plague, which was all too common in Marlowe's period. A modern variant is the suggestion that communism is God's punishment to the Orthodox Church for its lack of involvement.

For Marlowe, who later wrote about the Faust theme of selling a soul and ultimate retribution, the conqueror as God's scourge to the hypocritical was another broad subject. Because he presented it ironically – perhaps a mistake of youth – the point has often been missed.

To Kit Marlowe, who had seen the seminary at Rheims, a religious organization for education, used for fomenting war, the scourge of God theme was very relevant. Similarly he had known the Church to claim that the earth was flat, misquoting verses from the Old Testament and taking passages out of context to prove it. Exploration had now proved that the earth was round.

There is heavy irony in the betrayal of their Christian oaths by Baldwin and Frederick in *Tamburlaine*, Part Two, Act II. Their God did not give them victory because they had broken their oaths sworn in Christ's name. They were defeated by Orcanes, who had had strong words to say about perfidious Christians.

> Can there be such deceit in Christians,
> Or treason in the fleshy heart of man,
> Whose shape is figure of the highest God?
> Then, if there be a Christ, as Christians say,
> But in their deeds deny him for their Christ . . .

On his deathbed Tamburlaine asked for a map, and traced where he had marched with his conquering armies. He wished to see

> . . . how much
> Is left for me to conquer of all the world,
> That these, my boys, may finish all my wants . . .

> . . . what a world of ground
> Lies westward from the midst of Cancer's line
> Unto the rising of this earthly globe,
> Whereas the sun, declining from our sight,
> Begins the day with our Antipodes!
> And shall I die, and this unconquered!

In 1580, just seven years before these first performances of *Tamburlaine*, Francis Drake had returned from circumnavigating the world. He had established, even for the most reactionary, that the earth was a 'globe' and that the sun was lightening the southern hemisphere when the northern hemisphere was dark. Sir Francis Walsingham had, with the Queen, the Earl of Leicester, Sir Christopher Hatton and others, formed a syndicate to back Drake's voyage in 1577. Kit had no doubt heard from Thomas Walsingham exciting tales of Drake's travels, and was later to hear similar stories from Walter Raleigh. Narratives from Drake's sailors were still circulating and Kit's plays, mentioning distant countries, generated further excitement.

Although 1587 was the year in which the English were expecting the Armada, it was also the time when Walter Raleigh organized an expedition to found a colony in Virginia. Under the leadership of an artist, John White, whom Raleigh appointed governor, about one hundred and fifty people set out from Plymouth on 8 May. Raleigh, whom some have suggested was the model for Tamburlaine (though Marlowe met him too late for this to be the case), was typical of one kind of aspiring Renaissance man, anxious to expand knowledge in all directions. Watercolour paintings of Indians, found in Thomas Walsingham's home at the time of its demolition in the eighteenth century, may have been done by John White and have been relics of this Virginia expedition.

Kit Marlowe's *Tamburlaine*, staged seven years after Drake's circumnavigation of the world and the year before the Spanish Armada attacked England, caught the warlike feeling of the times and the excitement of the new learning and geographical discoveries, and was a spectacular success.

5 · 'The king of Spain's huge fleet'

The patron of the troupe for whom Kit Marlowe wrote most of his plays was Lord Howard, the Lord Admiral, and if friendship with the Walsinghams had played a part in selecting the acting company with whom both he and Tom Watson were involved, the Lord Admiral's was their likely choice. Lord Howard had been involved with the trials of Babington and of Mary Queen of Scots, and Sir Francis was responsible for both. Also Lord Howard commanded defence against the Armada, about the coming of which Sir Francis had warned.

Lord Howard was a rational man who saw sailors' illnesses as the result of lack of food rather than as visitations of God – an attitude that his troupe's leading playwright Kit Marlowe approved. On 28 May 1588 Lord Howard wrote to Lord Burleigh from Plymouth: 'My good Lord, there is here the gallantest company of captains, soldiers and mariners that I think was ever seen in England. It was a pity they should lack meat, when they are so desirous to spend their lives in her Majesty's service.'

While Queen Elizabeth was often mean in payment of her armed forces, of which this non-supplying of meat was one example, she could be remarkably kind in dealing face to face with sailors and soldiers. For example, in 1579 when she was travelling in her private barge between Deptford and Greenwich, a shot was fired across the river, striking one of the rowers. The Queen immediately gave the wounded man her scarf, saying he would 'want for nothing'. Such behaviour inspired the loyalty of her subjects, which was at its height in 1587 when *Tamburlaine* was first staged.

Sea captain Francis Drake, who also caught the imagination

of the people, was not similarly esteemed by the Spanish. Poet and playwright Lope de Vega, who sailed in the Armada, wrote that Drake was 'Satan himself, the incarnation of the Genius of Evil, the arch-enemy of the Church of God'. To Bernardino de Mendoza, a Spanish ambassador, Drake was 'the master thief of the unknown world'. Martin Frobisher, an Englishman, complained bitterly about 55,000 ducats Drake found in a crippled ship, *Nuestra Senora del Rosario*, in the course of the defence against the Armada. He stated: 'Drake thinks to cozen us of our shares in the loot, but we will have them, or I will make him spend the best blood in his belly.' If such random remarks about Drake were taken as seriously as some random comments about Marlowe, a different and wrong picture of the Elizabethan sea captain would emerge.

Marlowe's play *The Massacre at Paris* is set in the period from the massacre (1572) till 1590 (there is a reference to 'Sixtus's' bones, and Pope Sixtus died in 1590). So the Armada year is covered, from France, during the persecution of the Huguenots. The Duke of Guise, brother of Catholic kings Charles and Henry, led the persecution, putting loyalty to Philip of Spain and the Pope above loyalty to his brother the King of France. The result was his death, and the succession of Protestant Henry of Navarre, ally of Elizabeth of England, to the French throne.

There are many historically relevant quotations in Marlowe's *Massacre*:

Navarre: I'll muster up an army secretly,
          For fear that Guise, join'd with the king of Spain,
          Might seek to cross me in mine enterprise.

                                    (Act III, Scene i)

        ... Against the proud disturbers of the faith,
        (I mean the Guise, the Pope and king of Spain)
        Who set themselves to tread us under foot, ...

                                   (Act IV, Scene ii)

> And with the Queen of England join my force
> To beat the papal monarch from our lands,
> And keep those relics from our countries' coasts
>
> (Act IV, Scene iv)

Guise: Ay, and the Catholic Philip, king of Spain,
   Ere I shall want, will cause his Indians
   To rip the golden bowels of America.

> (Act IV, Scene v)

Henry: Did he not cause the king of Spain's huge fleet
   To threaten England, and to menace me?

> (Act V, Scene ii)

The line 'Philip and Parma, I am slain for you!' (in Act V, Scene ii) refers to the Duke of Parma, commander of the Spanish soldiers who were camped in the Low countries. They were planned to be transported to England by the Armada.

The Duke of Parma is also mentioned by Doctor Faustus (Act I, Scene i).

> I'll levy soldiers with the coin they bring,
> And chase the Prince of Parma from our land,
> And reign sole king of all the provinces.
> Yea, stranger engines for the brunt of war
> Than was the fiery keel at Antwerp's bridge
> I'll make my servile spirits to invent.

The 'fiery keel' was a fire ship used to destroy the Duke of Parma's bridge across the Scheldt in 1585. Fire ships were also used against the Armada in 1588 by Lord Howard.

The Massacre at Paris was to maintain its popularity with Elizabethan audiences for many years. In 1593, five years after the Armada's defeat, when the theatres reopened after the plague there were ten performances of *The Massacre at Paris* in five months. Four years later new properties were bought. These

49

included a long tawny cloak, embroidery for a hat, pairs of stock-ings, and 'a pair of silk stockings to play the Guise in'.

There is no direct evidence of Kit Marlowe's actions between the accident in the performance of *Tamburlaine*, Part Two, in November 1587 and the sword fight between Watson, Marlowe and Bradley in September 1589; but various activities, known to have taken place during his lifetime, must fall into this period. One is attendance at Raleigh's School of Night and another is initial work on *The Massacre at Paris*, though this was not staged until after *The Jew of Malta* and *Arden of Faversham*. Thirdly there was the Armada itself.

Was Kit Marlowe sent on a mission to France after the accident in *Tamburlaine*, Part Two? There were eight months between this and the sighting of the Armada in the next year. Sir Francis Walsingham would need to know when the Armada was due to sail, how many ships were involved, their size, and how many fighting men were on board. Numerous agents would be needed for Europe, and with his prior experience Kit was a likely choice. It would also earn him useful money.

In *The Massacre at Paris* (Act v, Scene v) King Henry says:

> Go call the English agent hither straight:
> I'll send my sister England news of this,
> And give her warning of her treacherous foes . . .
> Agent for England, send thy mistress word . . .

Kit's actually being an agent at a court was unlikely, but he was familiar with agents' work.

Another court rife with espionage in this period was that of James VI of Scotland. He encouraged poets, who mostly acted secretly as agents for one or other of the parties involved in the English succession. There is interesting speculation in this field as Kyd, in his letter to the Lord Keeper in 1593, said that Mar-lowe 'would persuade with men of quality to go unto the King of Scots, whither I hear Royden is gone, and where, if he had lived, he told me, when I saw him last, he meant to be'. Kit Marlowe was aware of activities in the Scottish Court.

The Armada itself had been planned in minute detail. It consisted of 20,000 sailors and soldiers, 130 ships and over 2,000 galley slaves, who manned the oars of the light galleys and heavy galleasses. They were mainly Turkish and Moorish – as in *Tamburlaine*, Part One, where two Moorish slaves draw the Turkish Emperor Bajazeth in his cage. The Spanish fleet, which thought of itself as a crusade against Protestant England and chanted prayers before battle that 'Our Lord might give us victory over the enemies of His Faith', was nevertheless cruel in employing Mohammedan slaves. The cruelty of Tamburlaine, the Scourge of God, against the Turks and Moors, is set in this historical context. Also aboard the Armada were 600 monks, priests and chaplains. The added weight of 2,630 great ordnance (heavy cannons) made the overladen fleet very unwieldy. The plan, that the Armada should rendezvous with the Duke of Parma and escort his troops from Flanders to England, appears always to have been doomed, but to the English then the approach of this great host must have been terrifying.

The English ships were sensibly smaller and nimbler, a feature that Hawkins and Sir Walter Raleigh had both championed. Raleigh explained (in *Excellent Observations and Notes concerning the Royall Navy and Sea-service*):

We find by experience that the greatest ships are least serviceable, go very deep to the water and of marvellous charge ... besides they are less nimble, less manageable and very seldom employed. 'Grande navio, grande fatiga; saith the Spaniard, a ship of 600 tons will carry as good ordnance as a ship of 1200 tons and ... the lesser will turn her broadside twice before the greater can wind once.

He continued, about the building of ships:

She should be strong-built, swift, stout-sided, that she carry out her guns all weathers, that the hull and try well, which we call a good sea-ship and that she stay well when boarding and turning on a wind is required.

Sailing ships of the Tudor period were at the mercy of prevailing winds, and while it is easy now to see that smaller ships would make quicker use of wind changes, at the time size was impressive. The English captains showed common sense in opting for smaller vessels; Drake's flagship the *Revenge*, for example, was only 500 tons.

Lord Howard arrived at Plymouth on 23 May with the main body of the Queen's ships to join the other vessels already assembled. Drake, Hawkins and Frobisher had all urged him to take the offensive and attack the Spanish in their own waters, but the weather was too bad for this course.

By 29 July the Spanish fleet was approaching the Scilly Isles. At dusk on the 31st the main body of English ships set sail out of Plymouth Sound, anchoring in the lee of Rame Head. Next morning the opposing fleets faced each other. The Spaniards unfurled their sacred Armada banner, and Lord Howard sent his pinnace to deliver a personal challenge to the Duke of Medina-Sidonia, admiral of the Armada.

Three nights before this Lord Howard had sent eight fireships among the Spanish ships in French waters, forcing some to cut their cables and collide. The next day (Monday, 29 July) there had been fighting at Gravelines, when much of the Armada's ammunition had been drawn. Victory was secured after the main confrontation, when the Spaniards were driven past the place where they had planned to rendezvous with the Duke of Parma.

Ill luck pursued the Spanish vessels. Many ships were destroyed off the coast of Ireland, and their crews and passengers were mostly drowned or killed by the Irish.

Bells pealed in England and bonfires blazed. There were triumphal processions.

During the battle the English had lost one hundred sailors and no ships, a tribute to their splendid seamanship. But many were now dying from illness contracted in the dreadful living conditions. Lord Howard wrote to Lord Burleigh on 10 August from Margate:

> My Good Lord, sickness and mortality begins wonderfully to grow amongst us, and it is a pitiful sight to see, here at Margate, how the men, having no place to receive them into here, die in the streets . . . It would grieve any man's heart to see them that have served so valiently to die so miserably.

In his plays after the *Tamburlaines* Marlowe did not glorify war. As he and Thomas Walsingham were Kent men, they would have heard of the disgraceful treatment of the sailors at Margate. Thoughts of the court of the Scots king, where men were honoured, would have been attractive then.

There was a service of national thanksgiving for deliverance from the Armada on 24 November at St Paul's Cathedral. Elizabeth rode there in her state coach with a canopy of a gilden crown. She was driven up Fleet Street and Ludgate Hill to the west door of the cathedral, through streets lined with thankful people.

So ended the Armada year. The exhilaration from England's victory was to continue, though there was disagreement about the non-payment of the victorious sailors and their shabby treatment.

Sadly for the Queen her favourite the Earl of Leicester had died on 4 September 1588, and he was remembered with kindness by the acting world for patronizing a company and building a theatre.

In 1588 Kit Marlowe worked on *The Massacre at Paris*, part of it probably for a court performance,* and the first part of *Doctor Faustus* – though the rest of the play was not finished until 1593. After the *Tamburlaines* his next play to be staged was *The Jew of Malta*. The Jew is so deeply rooted in Canterbury, in fact if not in title, that it is likely Kit visited his family in early 1589, and a performance of the play in Canterbury in 1592* may also

* See Chapter 10.

C

account for some of the references. *Arden of Faversham* could date from this time. The particular humour of this and *The Jew* suggests that Tom Watson was in Kit's company during early 1589 – and that he saw much of Tom Watson later this year is established by the swordfight.

In 1588 Queen Elizabeth had called her cousin Lord Hunsdon, who in his capacity as Lord Warden of the eastern marches resided for part of the year in Berwick, to London to take command of her bodyguard. Lord Hunsdon had had his own company of actors since 1564, to which James Burbage had once belonged, and his players became the Lord Chamberlain's Men when he was appointed to this office in 1585. His son, when he became Lord Chamberlain in 1597, was to continue the association with the theatre. This was the company for which Shakespeare did his later work. The Hunsdons had a third home, in Kent at the manor of Sevenoaks, and this Kentish circle included the Walsinghams and perhaps Thomas's protégé Kit Marlowe.

Diarist and astrologer Simon Forman, who later mentioned Thomas Walsingham for having an affair with a Mrs Webb of Canterbury, had also moved to London where he was to make interesting notes. In his entry for 1588 he wrote:

> ... This year I did thrive sufficient well, and had many friends; many enemies and troubles towards the latter end of the year ... it was the beginning of much sorrow and strife. I began to practice necromancy, and to call angels and spirits.

He was not alone in his recourse to angels and spirits – this became widespread, and was used for example in Kit Marlowe's *Doctor Faustus*. Forman had not yet reached fame as an astrological practitioner, and though he had avoided being called up for defence against the Armada he was pressed into service as a soldier for Portugal in the next year.

6 · The School of Night

Proof that the world was round, supplied by Magellan and Drake, was only part of the new information available to Marlowe's contemporaries in the 1580s.

The comfortable idea, derived from Aristotle, that the universe was a complex unity in which everything, human and environmental, formed a poetic whole was shaken by scientific discovery.

Medieval belief had been that matter was composed of four interacting elements and the heavens of a fifth immutable one; that the human body comprised four humours, which interacted for good or bad health; that there had been four ages of the world and the fifth, like the heavens, would be perfect and millennial; that the truth of these sets of four was underwritten by the four seasons, the four points of the compass, the four letters in the Hebrew name for God, and so on, Seven was also an operative number – there were seven deadly sins, seven cardinal virtues, seven sacraments of the Church, seven days of creation, seven ages of the life of man. The universe was seven concentric spheres of pure crystal which carried the planets in their orbits round the earth; and the state was part of this inter-related pattern – as the sun ruled the planets, so the king (or queen) ruled the state.

Kit Marlowe described part of such belief in Act II, Scene ii, of *Doctor Faustus*, adding Faustus's own doubts.

Faustus :   Speak, are there many spheres above the
                                              moon?
                         Are all celestial bodies but one globe,
                         As is the substance of this centric earth?

Mephistophilis: As are the elements, such are the heavens,
                  Even from the moon unto the empyrial orb,
                  Mutually folded in each other's spheres,
                  And jointly move upon one axel-tree,
                  Whose terminus is termed the world's wide
                                                      pole.
                  Nor are the names of Saturn, Mars or Jupiter
                  Feigned, but are erring stars . . .

Faustus: How many heavens or spheres are there?

Mephistophilis: Nine, the seven planets, the firmament and
                  the empyrial heaven.

Faustus: But is there not *coelum igneum* et *cristal-
                  lunum?*

Mephistophilis: No, Faustus, they be but fables.

Mephistophilis may not have been accurate in his information, but his ideas were not part of Aristotle's comfortable whole.

Queen Elizabeth did not frown on scientific experiment, and Walter Raleigh, one of the leaders of this movement, was among her favourites. A light-hearted example of his approach to experiment and the Queen's cooperation was when he wagered her that he could weigh smoke. He weighed tobacco before he smoked it in his pipe, and then weighed the ashes. The difference, he said, was the weight of smoke. The Queen paid up, remarking that she had known alchemists who could turn gold into smoke and Raleigh was the first to reverse the process.

Improved methods of measuring natural phenomena, followed by testing of observations, were uncovering new facts which appeared to shake the foundations of knowledge. Kit Marlowe, one of Raleigh's circle at the end of the 1580s, was reported as shocking rigid-minded people by frank logic. (This habit probably began in arguments with his outspoken family in Canterbury.)

The most subversive work in undermining the status quo of belief was done by the mathematician and astronomer Thomas

Hariot, who with Johannes Kepler demonstrated that the *primum mobile* (first mover), as it was then envisaged, could not exist. Hariot was one of Raleigh's circle for a long period. It had been believed that as the sun ruled the planets and the king the state, so God, in the guise of the *primum mobile*, ruled the empyrean realm of fire. His 'wheel' gave motion to the first sphere, which passed this to the second, and so the movement continued through the integrated universe. Hariot, roughly calculating the speed of the sun and moon, found that this prime mover would have to turn at incredible speed; Kepler estimated that it would travel at 7,500,000 miles in a twin pulse-beat, and simply could not exist. Ultimately Raleigh in his *History* denied that the prime mover, the crystalline heaven and the element of fire, existed at all. In 1593 Kit Marlowe was reported as saying that Moses was a mere juggler 'and that one Hariot, being Sir W. Raleigh's man, can do more than he'.

Marlowe described the heavens in Act III, Scene i, of *Doctor Faustus*, with classical overtones.

Chorus:　Learned Faustus,
To find the secrets of astronomy,
Graven in the book of Jove's high firmament,
Did mount him up to scale Olympus top . . .
He views the clouds, the planets and the stars,
The tropic, zones, and quarters of the sky,
From the bright circle of the horned moon,
Even to the height of Primum Mobile . . .

Thomas Hariot did useful work on symbols in algebra, and his most controversial contribution was calculating the chronology of the Old Testament. Having studied the time necessary for civilizations to rise and decay, he concluded that the Old Testament did not allow enough. Consequently he was accused of denying the word of God.

It was Raleigh and Hariot who endeavoured – with insufficient time to see the fruits of their labours – to found a civilization in

Virginia. Kit Marlowe has not commented on this experiment, though his enthusiasm for exploration and geographic expansion was demonstrated in *Tamburlaine*.

John Donne, yet to emerge as a leading literary figure, was soon to say that 'the new philosophy calls all in doubt' and to write different verse from Edmund Spenser, who was influenced by medieval concepts of idealized behaviour. Yet it was Spenser, both by chronology and friendship, who belonged to Raleigh's and Marlowe's circle at the end of the 1580s. This partially explains how Raleigh, with Marlowe, Hariot, poet George Chapman (renowned for translating Homer), and Walter Warner, could be interested in mysticism as well as scientific experiment. These Renaissance thinkers were prepared to accept the experience of mysticism while they discounted crystal spheres and empyrean fire. They were not atheists, though it was of this that they were accused. Donne, who was not a mystic, eventually underwent a conversion and died as Dean of St Paul's; both rationalism and less mystically idealized religion had developed quickly. Dr Dee, living a generation earlier, was feared by the superstitious as a sorcerer, though he made some scientific experiments; while the middle-men, Raleigh's School of Night (as later described by a phrase from Shakespeare's *Love's Labours Lost*), who were approaching gently to rationalist ideas, had the worst of both worlds, being accused of atheism while not attaining to untrammelled thinking.

Spenser was esteemed more highly by fellow poets, despite his medievalism, than Donne was to be. Kit Marlowe included some lines of Spenser's *The Fairie Queene* in his *Tamburlaine* plays, and it was Raleigh who brought Spenser back from Ireland to publish *The Fairie Queene* in London.

Several groups of lines appear both in Spenser's *Fairie Queene* and in Kit Marlowe's *Tamburlaine* plays. These include:

> Oh highest lamp of ever-living Jove,
> Accursed day, infected with my griefs,

Hide now thy stained face in endless night,
And shut the windows of the lightsome heavens . . .

Then let the stony dart of senseless cold
Pierce through the centre of my wither'd heart . . .

(Tamburlaine, Part One)

Like to an almond tree y-mounted high
Upon the lofty and celestial mount
Of ever-green Selinus, quaintly deck'd
With blossoms more white than Herycina's brows.

(Tamburlaine, Part Two)

It is not clear who influenced whom between Marlowe and Spenser. Spenser brought *The Fairie Queene* to London in 1589, and though the *Tamburlaines* were published in 1590 they had been acted since 1587. As Marlowe supervised the printing of the *Tamburlaines*, he must have read *The Fairie Queene*, or alternatively Spenser must have shown his poem to Marlowe or seen the *Tamburlaines* before the plays were printed. Presumably Walter Raleigh introduced the two poets to each other, or they met as mutual friends of Raleigh's.

Spenser's background compares interestingly with Kit Marlowe's. Edmund Spenser had entered Pembroke Hall, Cambridge, as a sizar – a poor student required to perform menial duties – in 1569. This was a decade ahead of Kit Marlowe who, due to his scholarship and unspecified means (money from spy duties, patronage from Thomas Walsingham, help from his uncle?), had been more affluent, if not as wealthy as some. Kit Marlowe was also of 'humble birth', i.e. not from a noble family, and neither was Gabriel Harvey, who became Spenser's friend but not Marlowe's. Nashe, another of humble birth and educated as a sizar, was to satirize Harvey in his pamphlets. Harvey, proud, quarrelsome, pedantic and of considerable intellect, was a critic of Raleigh's circle though he sometimes attended its discussions, and he approved of Spenser, whose friends apparently did not hold this against him. Spenser's father had been a journeyman in the cloth trade, by contrast with Marlowe's shoemaker father, who was his own master. Spenser received a good education at Merchant Taylor's School, which had been recently established under headmaster Richard Mulcaster. Here he learned literature as a living art, and received a solid grounding in Latin, Greek, Hebrew and French. 'Mery London, my most kindly Nurse', he later wrote in 'Prothalamion'. At Cambridge Spenser and Harvey came into contact with Puritanism, which was to influence them all their lives; Kit Marlowe and Nashe were not puritanically inclined. After working on the staff of the Earl of Leicester and there being influenced by the Earl's radiant nephew Sir Philip Sidney, Spenser moved to Ireland as secretary to the new Lord Deputy, Lord Grey of Wilton. He was still there, occupying the post of Clerk of the Council of Munster, when Raleigh found him in 1589. Raleigh was entranced by Spenser's poetry and brought him and the first three books of *The Fairie Queene* back to London. Though Spenser was an idealist with puritanical leanings he did not oppose the policy of ruthless oppression in Ireland. He was to spend much of his life among the Irish but was not sympathetic to them. He believed that Talus, in Book v of *The Fairie Queene*, was the right ruler for such a lawless, desolate, if beautiful country. The cruelty of Kit Marlowe's *Tamburlaine* was not out of place in such times.

In his first months in London Spenser met fellow poets among Raleigh's circle, and the Queen accepted his dedication of *The Fairie Queene*. But his reward, when it eventually came, was only a pension of £50. In his poem 'Mother Hubberd's Tale', he said 'how pitifull a thing is a Suters state'. It would seem that while the Queen smiled on him, Lord Burleigh did not, perhaps a legacy from his period with the Earl of Leicester. Back in Ireland in 1591 he continued with *The Fairie Queene* and also wrote an elegy for the Earl's dead nephew (and son-in-law of Sir Francis Walsingham) Philip Sidney, admiration for whose chivalry had become a cult. In Ireland in 1592 Spenser met Elizabeth

Boyle, whom he was to marry. He was to return to London in 1595 with three more books of *The Fairie Queene* and this time went to the Earl of Essex, another nephew of the now deceased Earl of Leicester, rather than to Raleigh, who was out of favour. He was back in Ireland for O'Neill's revolt in 1598, returning to London with dispatches in December 1598 and dying there a month later. Spenser was buried near Chaucer in Westminster Abbey, and other poets showed their respect by throwing their pens into his tomb. To the end this gentle poet of idealistic aspiration advocated ruthless action in Ireland. In 1596 he had written *View of the Present State of Ireland*, which was too blunt to be published until 1633. Some people placed him second to Chaucer as a great poet, though his work appears contrived next to that of Marlowe and Raleigh – and Nashe, who called him 'the Virgil of England'.

Compare the opening of *The Fairie Queene* with verses of Kit Marlowe's 'Come Live With Me and Be My Love', and Raleigh's 'reply'.

Lo! I, the man whose Muse whylome did maske,
As time her taught in lowly Shephards weeds,
Am now enforst, a farre unfitter taske,
For trumpets sterne to chaunge mine oaten reeds,
And sing of Knights and Ladies gentle deeds ...

(Spenser's *The Fairie Queene*)

Come live with me and be my love,
And we will all the pleasures prove
That valleys, groves, hills and fields,
Woods or steepy mountain yields ...

And I will make thee beds of roses,
And a thousand fragrant posies,
A cap of flowers, and a kirtle
Embroidered all with leaves of myrtle ...

(Marlowe)

If all the world and love were young,
And truth in every shepherd's tongue,
These pretty pleasures might me move,
To live with thee and be thy love . . .

Thy gowns, thy shoes, thy beds of roses,
Thy cap, thy kirtle and thy posies,
Soon break, soon wither, soon forgotten;
In folly ripe, in reason rotten . . .

(Raleigh)

Both the Renaissance and the new science seem a long way from 'Knights and Ladies gentle deeds', and Spenser's archaic writing does not appear contemporary with Marlowe's and Raleigh's easy cadences. But Spenser nevertheless included Virginia as one of the realms over which the Queen ruled in his dedication of 1596. By joining the discussions of Raleigh's group he showed up the new thinkers' modernity by contrast.

The cult of admiration for Philip Sidney's chivalry influenced another group of scholars with whom Raleigh's group was loosely related. This group became known as Rosicrucians, and their particular branch of chivalry still survives in the Rosicrucian Society and the Freemasons.

In 1577 young Philip Sidney had been sent on a mission to the Imperial court, to give the new emperor Rudolph II the condolences of Queen Elizabeth on the death of his father. Sidney visited the German Protestant princes on the way, to investigate the possibility of a Protestant League in Europe. Like his uncle the Earl of Leicester and his prospective father-in-law Sir Francis Walsingham, he believed in Protestant activism – that is, opposing Catholic countries like Spain before they attacked, rather than waiting to defend. Because the Queen would not sanction this course, Walsingham was driven to employing spies like Kit Marlowe to keep abreast of the news of Spain's gathering forces. When Sidney died and became a cult, the 'beau ideal' of Protestant chivalry associated with his memory was not only celebrated by the Queen's knights at Ascension Day tilts, but also spread to the Protestant German states. The Palatinate gave active support to Henry IV of France (whose initial victories were described in Kit Marlowe's *The Massacre at Paris*), thus putting Protestant activism into action. Another Englishman had become involved in Europe, moving from the Imperial court to Prague; this was the scientist and magus John Dee, who had been in court circles in England and become feared as a sorcerer (he was partially the model for Marlowe's *Doctor Faustus* and Shakespeare's Prospero in *The Tempest*). Both Protestant activism and Dee's mysticism were involved in Rosicrucianism.

A Rosicrucian book called *Naometria*, by Simon Studion, which used chronology as a basis for prophecy, described a meeting of Protestant rulers against the Catholic League in 1586, two years before the Armada attacked England; the leaders allegedly attending were Henry of Navarre, Queen Elizabeth and the King of Denmark. The year 1586 was the one in which Queen Elizabeth's armies intervened in the Netherland under Philip Sidney's uncle the Earl of Leicester. John Dee and his associate Edward Kelley were in Bohemia – the home of the Hussite 'heresy' which interested Kit Marlowe and his friends – at various times between 1583 and 1589; where also went Hariot's correspondent Johannes Kepler and Giordano Bruno, whose works had influenced Thomas Watson and Sir Francis Walsingham.

Though Raleigh's 'School' were interested in science and a species of rationalism, they were also, by association with Spenser and through their Protestant and esoteric connections, involved with Rosicrucian arts, including the magico-scientific ones of alchemy and spirit-summoning. Hence Kit Marlowe's *Doctor Faustus*, which was written in two parts – some in 1588–9 when the German version of the *Faust* book first became available, and the rest in 1592–3 when an English translation of the Faust book appeared.

It is easier to understand how these differing discussion subjects of Raleigh's group – scientific, mystic, Protestant – came together, when the participants are seen in historical context. The Armada had been feared, had arrived, and another attack was half-expected.

Protestantism became patriotism for the politically involved Raleigh and members of Walsingham's circle. In a time when Spenser was honoured above Donne, and the traditional was more appreciated than the innovatory, new scientific experiment could seem like old alchemy and be similarly feared, and studied. Hence Raleigh's group, discussing both, were criticized for both. The crowds who burned John Dee's library did it as much against his scientific experiments as his magical books. An enlighteningly cynical picture of Raleigh's 'School' is given in John Aubrey's *Brief Life* of Thomas Hariot, written in the seventeenth century.

Mr Hariot went with Sir Walter Ralegh into Virginia, and haz writt the *Description of Virginia,* which is printed. Dr. Pell tells me that he finds amongst his papers, an Alphabet that he had contrived for the American Language, like Devills . . .

Sir Francis Stuart had heard Mr Hariot say that he had seen nine Cometes, and had predicted Seaven of them, but did not tell them how. 'Tis very strange: *excogitent Astronomi.*

He did not like (or valued not) the old storie of the Creation of the World. He could not beleeve the old position; he would say *ex nihilo nihil fit* [nothing comes to nothing]. But a *nihilum* killed him at last: for in the top of his Nose came a little red speck (exceeding small) which grew bigger and bigger, and at last killed him. I suppose it was that which the Chirurgians call a *noli me tangere.*

He made a Philosophical Theologie, wherin he cast-off the Old Testament, and then the New-one would (consequently) have no Foundation. He was a Deist. His Doctrine he taught to Sir Walter Raleigh, Henry Earle of Northumberland, and some others. The Divines of those times look't on his manner of death as a Judgement upon him for nullifying the Scripture.

The 'some others' covers an interesting group including, in the 1580s and 1590s, Kit Marlowe.

In an excerpt from Marlowe's *Doctor Faustus*, in Act IV, Scene

64

vii, apart from clowning-about references to Faustus's trick wooden leg, there are two characteristic features. The first is the presence of the Duke of Vanholt (Anholt) one of the Protestant German princes approached by Philip Sidney, and later a leader of Protestant activism; and the other is the geography lesson given when the Duke's pregnant wife asks for a bunch of grapes.

Duke: This makes me wonder more than all the rest, that at this time of year, when every tree is barren of his fruit, from whence you had these ripe grapes.

Faustus: Please it your grace, the year is divided into two circles over the whole world, so that when it is winter with us, in the contrary circle it is likewise summer with them, as in India, Saba, and such countries that lie East, where they have fruit twice a year. From whence, by means of a swift spirit that I have, I have these grapes brought as you see.

A picture of the period can be gained from *Doctor Faustus*; and that Kit Marlowe was a participant in wide-ranging discussions is clear from the number of topical references in the play, and the way the subjects are treated.

For example, from Act I, Scene i:

> ... Be a physician, Faustus: heap up gold
> And be eternized for some wondrous cure ...
> ... Are not thy bills hung up as monuments,
> Whereby whole cities have escaped the plague ...
> These necromantic books are heavenly,
> Lines, circles, scenes, letters and characters ...
> ... All things that move between the quiet poles
> Shall be at my command ...

In the play, Doctor Faustus plumps wholeheartedly for magic.

> ... Philosophy is odious and obscure
> Both law and physic are for petty wits.

> Divinity is basest of the three,
> Unpleasant, harsh, contemptible and vile.
> 'Tis magic, magic that hath ravished me.

After Faustus has agreed to trade his soul with Mephistophilis, Mephistophilis makes comments which mirror the 'heresy' of the period:

> Hell hath no limits, nor is circumscribed
> In one self place. But where we are is hell,
> And where hell is there we must ever be.

There is also a surprisingly modern comment on marriage.

> Tut, Faustus, marriage is but a ceremonial toy.

In Act II, Scene i, Mephistophilis and Faustus dabble in humanism:

> But thinkst thou heaven is such a glorious thing?
> I tell thee, Faustus, it is not half so fair
> As thou or any man that breathes on earth ...

And there is a reference to the poet Homer who was translated by George Chapman, another of Raleigh's circle at that time, who was to complete Marlowe's *Hero and Leander*:

> ... Have I not made blind Homer sing to me
> Of Alexander's love and Oenon's death?
> And hath not he that built the walls of Thebes
> With ravishing sound of his melodious harp
> Made music with my Mephistophilis?

The first part of *Doctor Faustus* is important for establishing Kit Marlowe's presence among the 'talkers' in 1588-9.

7 · Norton Folgate

In September 1589 Kit Marlowe was involved in a swordfight in the outer London district of Norton Folgate. He was attacked by William Bradley, an enemy of Thomas Watson and his in-laws the Swift family. The affair was to have considerable influence on Kit. His subsequent days in Newgate prison underwrote his maturing as playwright and poet.

Kit must have resided in the Norton Folgate area from soon after his arrival in London, if Tom Watson took him immediately in hand. Watson was then resident near Bishopsgate as tutor to William Cornwallis's son, and outside Bishopsgate were the Theatre and the Curtain playhouses.

In his *Survey of London*, prepared towards the end of the sixteenth century, John Stow described Norton Folgate as it was in Kit Marlowe's time. 'North, and by east from Bishopsgate', Stow wrote, was a wide street with the parish church of St Buttolph on the west side. Next to it was the hospital of St Mary of Bethlehem which had been founded by a citizen of London. Then outside 'the bars' was 'Norton fall gate', which belonged to the Dean of St Paul's. So Norton Folgate was a few minutes walk up a wide road from Bishopsgate.

Stow had a lot to say about Hog Lane, the street where the fight was to take place. It stretched north towards St Mary Spittle from Bishopsgate, and until forty years previously had had hedge-rows of elm trees on both sides, with bridges and stiles for people to climb over into the surrounding fields where they could walk, 'recreate and refresh their dull spirits in the sweet and wholesome air'. But recently garden-houses, small cottages, tenter yards and

67

bowling alleys, had spread over the whole area, from Houndsditch in the west to beyond Whitechapel in the east.

Stow returned to Hog Lane later in his *Survey*, with some bitterness. The common fields ought to be open to the citizens, he claimed, and all men should be free to walk there. But 'filthy cottages, . . . inclosures, and laystalls' . . . had encroached on this pleasant place. Acts of parliament and proclamations to the contrary had been ignored. Some parts of Hog Lane were so crowded that there was scarcely room for carriages and droves of cattle to pass each other. It was a 'blemish' on London to have this entry passage deteriorate in such an 'unsavoury and unseemly' manner.

The purpose of Bishopsgate, Stow claimed, was for the use of travellers to and from Norfolk, Suffolk and Cambridgeshire. So Kit may, on his journey from Cambridge, have called on Tom Watson before he entered London proper, if he came from Cambridge by way of Bishopsgate.

Stow did not blame the theatres for the decline of the Bishopsgate district. His only reference to them was that 'comedies, tragedies, interludes, and histories', true and imagined, were now being staged, and that the Theatre and the Curtain had been built to house them.

Stow told a story about Bishopsgate that throws some light on the feelings in Tudor times against foreign merchants, which was to have consequences for Thomas Kyd, and Kit Marlowe, in 1593. Several centuries before, Henry III had accorded rights and privileges to some merchants of the Haunce, who maintained a building in London named Guildhalla Theutonicorum. These rights and privileges were confirmed by Edward I, but ten years later were said to include the upkeep of Bishopsgate. The merchants accepted this and an Alderman of the Haunce, one Gerard Marbod, with the merchants, granted two hundred and ten marks sterling for the gate's repair, and guaranteed that it would be done again from time to time. The gate was rebuilt in 1479, and the same was planned for 1551, when the merchants had already purchased new stone. However such was the feeling of the English merchants against foreign ones, that the rights and privileges of the Haunce merchants were withdrawn altogether before the gate could be finished, and, said Stow, the old gate was still there.

The Jew of Malta (written in 1588–9) shows Kit Marlowe as less enthusiastic about life than the optimistic young writer of *Tamburlaine*, and this is understandable when the reality of Norton Folgate is compared with the aspirations of Canterbury and Cambridge. Because of the success of the theatre from Marlowe's time till now, its quiet beginning is often forgotten, and also its meagre returns. There were no royalties, and a playwright without a company to sell his plays to had no livelihood.

The small amount of space allotted to the theatre in Stow's *Survey* – even small within his 'Sports and Pastimes' section– suggests that the theatre was relatively small fry for many people. It needed to be a commercial success to survive, which Kit Marlowe's plays were; and Marlowe's plays went on drawing big houses for years after Shakespeare became leading playwright with the Lord Chamberlain's Men. The *élan* which Marlowe's, and Shakespeare's, plays evoked came as much from patriotism (because of the threat from Spain) as from appreciation of their words. Another time when Britain has been threatened with imminent invasion, the Second World War, brought a similar renaissance in the British theatre, which then included films. Shakespeare's *Henry V*, for example, had phenomenal success as a film just after the Second World War, and there were many successful new plays.

By 1589 Kit Marlowe had discovered that writing for the theatre was demanding work, not liberation. He had caught the feeling of the time in *Tamburlaine*, and had to go on catching it to remain financially secure, as there was little chance for spying to supplement his income once the Armada had been defeated. That Kit Marlowe did remain solvent is shown by the jealousy of impecunious playwrights like Greene and Nashe. Memories of the Marlowe family's moves caused by non-payment of rent, and the inheritance of prudence from his mother, prompted Kit to avoid in Cambridge the poverty suffered by Spenser and Nashe, and to remain solvent in London. Marlowe's 'luck' contained elements of prudence and hard work. Greene, living in poverty in a tenement after a distinguished university career just past, was very jaundiced about Kit's success, and the former's comments are often not understood in this context. Shakespeare, who was also financially prudent, was similarly unpopular with less successful playwrights. Nevertheless, for Kit Marlowe too conditions in Norton Folgate were less congenial than in the clean air of Cambridge. There was little open sky in London, and the stars are hardly mentioned in his plays after the spangled *Tamburlaines*.

Kit's new cynicism was a development of his grand irony of *Tamburlaine* applied to particular cases:

Barabas: Well fare the Arabians, who so richly pay . . .
The needy groom, that never finger'd groat,
Would make a miracle of thus much coin . . .

(The Jew of Malta, Act I)

A kingly kind of trade, to purchase towns
By treachery, and sell 'em by deceit?

(Act v)

There are more references to the Kent countryside in *The Jew of Malta* than in any other of Kit's plays, except for *Arden of Faversham*, and in crowded London Kit began to appreciate Kent. He may have made a visit home in the spring, riding there through the awakening countryside and may even have been accompanied by Tom Watson. Kit would have taken his friend out of London to separate him from the Swift family's vendetta with William Bradley – though if this were the case he was not successful, as it was Kit himself whom Bradley was to attack, and Watson who was to strike the fatal blow when he rescued Kit.

An example of Tom Watson's mocking type of humour in *The Jew of Malta* is the scene in which Barabas, disguised as a French musician with a lute and a nosegay in his hat, serenades Ithamore,

Bellamira and Pilia-Borza, and poisons them with the scent of the nosegay; and such a scene would have been influenced by Watson's humour if Kit had been continually in his company.

Ithamore:	Dost not know a Jew, one Barabas?
Barabas:	Very mush: monsieur, you no be his man?
Pilia-Borza:	His man?
Ithamore:	I scorn the peasant: tell him so.
Barabas (aside):	He knows it already.
Ithamore:	'Tis a strange thing of that Jew: he lives upon pickled grasshoppers and sauced mushrooms.
Barabas (aside):	What a slave's this! The Governor feeds not as I do.
Ithamore:	He never put on a clean shirt since he was circumcised.
Barabas (aside):	O rascal; I change myself twice a-day.
Ithamore:	The hat he wears, Judas left under the elder when he hanged himself.
Barabas (aside):	'Twas sent me for a present from the Great Cham.
Pilia-Borza:	A nasty slave he is. – Whither now, fiddler?
Barabas:	Pardonnez-moi, monsieur; me be no well.

In the spring, it seemed, few of the clouds of the coming autumn tragedy were in sight. Marlowe (and Watson?), riding down the Kentish lanes on a leisurely journey to Canterbury, were heartened by the scene.

Ithamore:	. . . Where painted carpets o'er the meads are hurl'd,
	And Bacchus' vineyards overspread the world;
	Where woods and forests go in goodly green . . .
	The meads, the orchards, and the primrose-lanes . . .

There is a speech by Ithamore, like a black echo of the Canterbury pilgrims.

> One time I was an hostler in an inn,
> And in the night time secretly would I steal
> To travellers' chambers, and there cut their throats.
> Once at Jerusalem, where the pilgrims kneel'd,
> I strewed powder on the marble stones,
> And therewithall their knees would rankle so,
> That I have laugh'd a-good to see the cripples
> Go limping home to Christendom on stilts.
>
> (Act II, Scene iii)

In the last part of *The Jew of Malta*, Kit Marlowe made good use of the improved stagecraft available in buildings constructed for plays, which he had had time to examine in detail after the earlier introductions from Tom Watson, the success of his own *Tamburlaine* and the hiatus following the temporary closure after the incident in *Tamburlaine*, Part Two.

When plays had been produced in inn yards or on open stages in public, it had been difficult to allow for two settings in one scene – except when there was a balcony over an inn yard, as at the inn now called the Eagle,* opposite Corpus Christi at Cambridge. The Eagle has had its balcony restored, but records confirm that it possessed an actors' gallery when Kit was at Corpus Christi. Balconies such as this provided for an upper and lower level, and actors on the balcony could pretend not to see those below if the story demanded it. Simultaneous activity could also take place on both levels. So when the theatres were built the balcony was kept as part of the stage and therefore three sections – front of stage, balcony, and a curtained-off area under the balcony – were available for use. In the *Jew of Malta* (and

---

* The history of the Eagle is included in *The City of Cambridge, a Survey and Inventory by the Royal Commission on Historical Monuments*, Her Majesty's Stationery Office, 1959.

The Massacre at Paris) two settings, and sometimes three, were
used in single scenes.

In Act II, Scene i, Barabas enters on the front section of the
stage with a lantern. Abigail soon appears on the balcony. Place
and time are thus set. Barabas is outside the nunnery, and Abigail
in it. This is the scene in which she throws the bags of gold to
her father.

When the curtains open in the cauldron scene, Barabas is on
the upper level 'with a hammer, very busy; and carpenters'; he
tests cords, hinges, cranes and pulleys. The carpenters depart,
and the governor arrives. Barabas then explains his plot. He will
invite 'Calymath and his consorts' into the gallery, and pull a
cable so they would fall through the upper level into a cauldron
concealed under the floor beneath. Calymath enters on the lower
level and is invited to 'ascend our homely stairs'. But the governor
intervenes; he cuts the cable so that *Barabas* falls through the
gallery and hurtles into the cauldron. Great theatre, in which
Ned Alleyn made a tremendous impression.

The Marlowe/Bradley/Watson swordfight, though looming from
Watson's point of view all the summer, happened suddenly.

Bradley was the son of an innkeeper of Gray's Inn Lane,
Holborn, and the disagreement had begun when he did not pay
a debt of £14 owed to another innkeeper, John Alleyn, brother
of Ned Alleyn who starred in Kit Marlowe's plays. Hugo Swift,
Watson's brother-in-law, legally represented John Alleyn, who
threatened to bring a suit against William Bradley in the Court
of Common Pleas. Bradley's acquaintances George Orrell threatened that if Hugo Swift took the matter to court he would be
physically attacked. Swift appealed to the Queen's bench for
securities of the peace against George Orrell. However, Swift,
with his brother-in-law Tom Watson and John Alleyn, took action
anyway because of Orrell's known belligerent character. (He later
fought in Ireland under Lord Monteagle, and played a prominent
part in the Earl of Essex's rebellion when 'he did run and

leap in the forefront with Sir Christopher Blunt and Mr Bushell, their weapons drawn, crying 'Saw, saw, saw, saw, tray, tray'.)* Bradley countered with a petition against Hugo Swift, John Alleyn and Thomas Watson. Bradley also took action. On the afternoon of 18 September at about two-thirty, when he was walking along Hog Lane, he saw Kit Marlowe. Marlowe was a friend of the offending Watson, and John Alleyn's brother acted in his plays. Bradley attacked him.

Kit defended himself. Watson approached soon after and hastily intervened. He was over-zealous and Bradley was killed. The crowd who had gathered testified that Bradley had shouted, 'Arte thowe nowe come then I will have a boute with thee' to Watson. Nevertheless Stephen Wylde, a tailor of Norton Folgate and part-time constable, took Watson and Marlowe before Sir Owen Hopton, justice of the district and Lieutenant of the Tower. As they had been arrested on suspicion of murder they were placed in Newgate prison. A dramatic climax to the feud between Watson's family, Ned Alleyn's brother, and William Bradley.

Was the swordfight in Shakespeare's *Romeo and Juliet* based on this incident, as some suggest? It by no means parallels it. Certainly Tybalt, who could be taken to represent Bradley, first attacked Romeo, but verbally only. It is Mercutio who draws:

Mercutio:	O calm, dishonourable, vile submission! Alla stoccata carries it away. (Draws.) Tybalt, you rat-catcher, will you walk.
Tybalt:	What wouldst thou have with me?
Mercutio:	Good king of cats, nothing but one of your nine lives, that I mean to make bold withal, and, as you shall use me hereafter, dry-beat the rest of the eight. Will you pluck your sword out of his pilcher by the ears?

* Letter from William Reynolds to Robert Cecil (Cecil papers at Hatfield House).

> make haste, lest mine be about your ears
> ere it be out.

Tybalt (drawing):   I am for you.

Thus far there is resemblance to the Norton Folgate fight, except that Mercutio was first on the scene, which according to the inquest was not the case with Watson. But is the inquest the full story? Watson must have frequented Norton Folgate often. And while Watson was one of the three named in Bradley's petition, Bradley might consciously have chosen Marlowe to attack because he was less adept at swordplay than Watson, Swift or John Alleyn. Kit was certainly younger than them, and Bradley *did* attack him first, even if he shouted, 'arte thowe nowe come then I will have a boute with thee' when Watson arrived. Tybalt's 'I am for you' to Mercutio is the nearest point of similarity between the two stories.

After that they diverge. Tybalt mortally wounds Mercutio. In the Bradley affray, Watson is wounded but does not die. However he did spend weary months in Newgate prison, compared with Kit's brief stay, and was a shadow of his former self when he emerged, ultimately dying in 1592. The real difference is that Romeo, stung by the death of his friend Mercutio, kills Tybalt.

There are several possibilities about the question of whether Shakespeare had the Bradley fight in mind in this scene in *Romeo and Juliet*. The inquest need not have been the full truth. Inquests rarely are. Then if Shakespeare had heard the story by hearsay, he may have got some of the details wrong. Shakespeare was adapting the story of Romeo and Juliet, not the life of Marlowe, and such a scene would anyway be part of the Romeo and Juliet story line, not an inserted thumbnail documentary of an incident of several years before. What does seem likely is that Shakespeare, who was a suggestible writer, did think of Marlowe and Watson when a swordfight came into the story. The character of Mercutio bears resemblance to Watson. Whether Romeo tells us much about Kit Marlowe is less likely.

8 · Newgate

The inquest on William Bradley was held next day, 19 September, when the Middlesex county coroner, Ion Chalkhill, presided. Evidence was brought that Thomas Watson killed Bradley in self-defence. The jurors decided Bradley's death was 'not by felony', and Watson and Marlowe were to await the Queen's pardon.

Kit Marlowe was allowed bail from 1 October. Two men, 'Richard Kytchine of Clifford's Inn, gentleman, and Humfrey Rowland of East Smithfield, horner', stood surety of twenty pounds each. He was bound over in the sum of forty pounds, had to appear at the next Sessions to answer anything alleged against him, and could not depart without permission of the court. Kitchin practised law at Clifford's Inn, and later appeared as Philip Henslowe's legal representative. In 1600 he was to give evidence on behalf of the Mermaid Tavern's host, William Williamson, in a Star Chamber case. Humphrey Rowland was a constable of East Smithfield and 'a maker of Lanterne hornes', who stood surety for people on a number of occasions.

As Kit Marlowe's bail was from 1 October, he waited almost a fortnight in Newgate prison. Until this time, apart from the threat to withhold his MA at Cambridge, he had not been in trouble, and though there had been jealousy of the success of *Tamburlaine*, records even of this came mainly after the Newgate episode. Earlier his family had moved because of non-payment of rent, and he had been a spy, but these were less disturbing than this fatal affray, which he had not anticipated. If Norton Folgate was disappointing after Cambridge, Newgate was the nadir of existence.

Richard Baines in 1593, supporting Kyd's accusations when Marlowe was charged with atheism, referred to this episode. Baines claimed that Marlowe learned to make counterfeit coins in Newgate from 'poole a prisoner in newgate who hath greate Skill in mixture of mettals'. Baines alleged that Kit claimed he had 'as good Right to Coine as the Queen of England . . . (and) ment through help of a Cunninge stamp maker to Coin ffrench Crownes, pistolets and English shillinges'.

Marlowe and Watson escaped the worst rigours of Newgate as their friends could afford to bribe the jailers. This was the custom of the time. The 'boozing ken' was one haunt of 'privileged' prisoners in Newgate. However, even the privileged did not escape the squalor. In 'The Blacke Dogge of Newgate' (published 1600) Luke Hutton wrote of his experience there.

> A rat doth rob the candle from my handes,
> And then a hundred rats all sallie forth . . .
> Whilst thus I lay in irons under ground,
> I heard a man that begged for releese:
> And in a chaine or iron was he bound . . .
> Begging one penny to buie a hundred bread
> Hungered and stervd, for want of food ny dead . . .

It was a cruel age in terms of punishment; hanging, drawing and quartering was the normal method of execution for traitors. Hanging was a spectacle much enjoyed by crowds, who flocked to Tyburn, the site of the public hangman (near the area now called Marble Arch). This enjoyment of public hanging explains why the plays in this period contained so much bloodshed and violence.

Newgate prison was an example of the cruelty of the age. Apart from the general appalling conditions and tortures used, the cell reserved for condemned prisoners, 'limbo', was completely in darkness, a space with no window over the prison gate. Residence there before hanging shocked condemned prisoners into numbness. One improvement of Elizabethan times was that there were fewer deaths by burning than in Mary's reign, though burning for heresy still occurred, as in the case of Francis Kett. Newgate prison did not alter much during several Tudor reigns.

What Kit saw in Newgate is reflected in additions to *The Jew* and *The Massacre,* and in *Edward II* and *Doctor Faustus.* For example, from *Doctor Faustus*:

> Now, Faustus, let thine eyes with horror stare
> Into that vast perpetual torture-house.
> There are the furies tossing damned souls
> On burning forks.

And from *Edward II* :

> This usage makes my misery increase.
> But can my air of life continue long,
> When all my senses are annoy'd with stench?
> Within a dungeon England's King is kept,
> Where I am starv'd for want of sustenance.

Fastidious Kit, who had known the refinements of Cambridge and the grand house of his patron Thomas Walsingham, found Newgate prison most unpleasant.

On 3 December Kit Marlowe appeared at the assizes, where Richard Kitchen and Humphrey Rowland stood surety for him. One of the Judges of Assize was a Kentishman, Sir Roger Manwood, Chief Baron of the Exchequer. When Manwood died in December 1592, Kit wrote a Latin epitaph for him, probably commissioned, though perhaps it was Kit's gratitude for his acquittal. This epitaph was discovered in a 1629 edition of *Hero and Leander,* on the back of the title page, with Marlowe's name subscribed. It also appeared twice in the commonplace book of a young contemporary of Kit's called Henry Oxinden, who lived at Barham, a few miles outside Canterbury. Translated, it reads:

On the death of this most honourable man, Roger Manwood,
Knight,

Chief Baron of the Queen's Exchequer.

Terror of the night vagrant, stern scourge of the profligate,

Speedy Alcides, and destroyer of the obdurate thief,

Is buried within the urn. Rejoice ye sons of iniquity!

Mourn, innocent one, with hair dishevelled on your sorrowful
head!

The light of the courts, the glory of the ancient law is dead;

Alas, much virtue has gone out with him to the barren shores

Of the nether world. So many virtues had he

United in one man; do not profane the remains

Of one whose glance made thousands tremble.

And so when the messenger of bloody death strikes you

May your bones rest happily in peace

And may they outlive the monuments of the tomb! *

Fulsome words, particularly as rumour suggested that the judge was not averse to bending the law. Kit was fortunate to have both Manwood, and Fleetwood, who later bought a copy of *Tamburlaine*, on the bench on this occasion.

Nevertheless, Newgate was the turning point of Kit's life, though he was exonerated. As well as the shattering effect of residence in this terrifying prison, when Kit emerged he no longer had the company of Thomas Watson, who was still in Newgate. If Kit had the protection of Thomas Watson from the moment he arrived in London, then he was now alone for the first time and a prey to less benevolent company.

* This translation is by A. J. P. Taylor and the author.

9 · Blood Guilt

Kit Marlow was now twenty-five years old. He had been in London for more than two years and had achieved success in a risky business – the new theatres. What kind of person had he become? At Canterbury he had been a clever, imaginative boy saved from working in his father's shop by scholarships to King's School and Cambridge University. At Cambridge he had graduated with two degrees and become a spy in the pre-Armada period for the Walsinghams, making important friends and gaining bizarre experience. In London, though not prominently connected, he had known prominent people. Both *Tamburlaines* had been successful. Then the disaster at Hog Lane, a short stay in Newgate prison, and time for Kit to take stock . . .

After 1588 scares were to occur that Spain was preparing for another attack on England. The euphoria, following the defeat of the Armada, became national awareness fostered by defence. Though Kit was to be drawn into writing nationalist plays, his immediate thoughts in 1589 were mainly of farce and tragedy; none of his plays now had the optimism and adolescent idealism of *Tamburlaine*.

His *élan* which had survived the transition to London and was poured into *Tamburlaine*, Part Two, now lacked illusion. *The Jew of Malta*, *The Massacre at Paris*, and possibly *Arden of Faversham* were tragedy, farce and ironic topical comment.

Kit had become a man of the world. He is nearest to Shakespeare in keeping his own counsel, though hearsay comments about him appeared, and people who allege that Marlowe 'was' Shakespeare err in supposing them different types of person, as the two had much in common. Both from middle-class stock, they had

middle-class financial prudence and they succeeded in the professional theatre. Shakespeare may have benefited from Marlowe's
disappearance, but there would have been room for both had
Marlowe remained in London after 1593.

Kit differed from Shakespeare in being better educated and
more dependent on external stimuli. It is possible that one of
Kyd's comments in 1593, about Scotland, concerned external
stimuli. Kyd wrote that Marlowe had stated he was going to
Scotland, and while this is a hearsay statement, it may, like the
story of the counterfeiter in Newgate prison cited by Richard
Baines, have a grain of truth. Thoughts of the Scottish court may
have attracted Kit after his release from Newgate, because poets
were honoured there. King James was in fact to keep up his
patronage of poets after he ascended the English throne in 1603,
and had been involved with them as early as the 1580s when
he formed a friendship with Philip Sidney, even writing an
impressive sonnet on Sidney's death, which he later published.

There is a unity of theme between the Scottish tragedy
Macbeth, Marlowe's *The Massacre at Paris*, and *Arden of
Faversham* – designing evil women and blood guilt. In the case
of *The Massacre* and, possibly, *Arden*, Marlowe's own experience
of the death of Bradley may have influenced him, though some
of *The Massacre* was written before the Hog Lane tragedy.
Macbeth, because it flattered King James, who was a descendant
of Banquo, by saying that Banquo's descendants would inherit,
is an interesting case. Taken mainly from historical chronicles by
Holinshed, it is the only Scottish play to survive from its decade.
The blood guilt theme in *Arden* may have made playwrights
notice the *Macbeth* story's theme when Scottish material in
James's favour was being sought, Shakespeare's later version becoming standard. Chettle with some other playwrights tried to
compose a Scottish play in the 1590s, without success.

At the end of 1589, after Kit's release and acquittal, his life
broadened. *Arden of Faversham* reflects the mixture of tragedy
and farce in his outlook, and his *The Massacre at Paris* had a

dominating woman causing murder – Queen Catherine, the blood-thirsty Queen Mother of France. Queen Catherine's character was made clear at the start.

> Charles: Come mother,
> Let us go to honour this solemnity.
> Catherine (aside): Which I'll dissolve with blood and cruelty.

Arden of Faversham is a simple, almost farcical story, set in Marlowe's native Kent, telling of Alice Arden's plan to incite others to murder her husband so that she can marry her lover Mosbie. Ultimately the murder of Arden succeeds, after many false attempts by an ever-growing army of murderers, but Alice is overcome by remorse, in the manner of Lady Macbeth. She cannot wash the blood away: 'The more I strive, the more the blood appears.'

The play begins by establishing her deceitful character. She speaks lovingly to Arden.

> Husband, what mean you to get up so early?
> Summer nights are short, and yet you rise ere day.
> Had I been wake, you had not risen so soon.

Soon she is speaking lovingly to Mosbie, and of Arden as though he were the Jew of Malta.

> Nay, Mosbie, let me still enjoy thy love,
> And happen what will, I am resolute.
> My saving husband hoards up bags of gold
> To make our children rich, and now is he
> Gone to unload the goods that shall be thine . . .

To Greene, one of the people she incites to murder Arden, Alice tells a wildly untrue tale.

> Ah, Master Greene, be it spoken in secret here,
> I never live good day with him alone;
> When he's at home, then have I froward looks,

> Hard words and blows to mend the watch withal;
> And though I might content as good a man,
> Yet doth he keep in every corner trulls . . .

Eventually she deludes herself, when Mosbie becomes less ardent.

> I know he loves me well, but dares not come,
> Because my husband is so jealous,
> And these my narrow-prying neighbours blab,
> Hinder our meetings when we would confer . . .

After chases in Kent and London, and attempts by Alice herself to administer poison, Arden is finally murdered. Then Alice, like Lady Macbeth, suffers from blood guilt and the delusion that her hands can never be cleansed.

Alice: And, Susan, fetch water and wash away this blood.
Susan: The blood cleaveth to the ground and will not out.
Alice: But with my nails I'll scrape away the blood; –
    The more I strive, the more the blood appears!
    . . . In vain we strive, for here his blood remains.

The play of *Macbeth* was influenced by *Arden*'s female blood guilt scene. Not only were the two scenes similar, but Holinshed, which was the main source for *Macbeth*, had made little of Lady Macbeth, and even less of her remorse. The Holinshed chronicle also dealt with the murder of Duff by Donwald, who was encouraged by his wife, though again there was no mention of her remorse. The killing of King Duncan in Shakespeare's play was more like Donwald's actions than Macbeth's.

After the murder, 'a mysterious voice chastised him [Donwald] . . . It shall come to passe, that both thou thy self, and thy issue, through the just vengeance of almightie God, shall suffer worthie punishment, to the infamie of thy house and thy family for evermore . . . The King with this voice being striken into great dread and terror, passed that night without anie sleepe coming to his eies'. This appeared in Shakespeare's play as:

Methought I heard a voice cry 'Sleep no more!
Macbeth doth murder sleep!'

Lady Macbeth's blood guilt speeches were moving in Shakespeare's play, yet while they bear a resemblance to Alice Arden's inability to remove Arden's blood, they bear none to the original stories in Holinshed, and thus apparently link the two plays.

Though Banquo's kinship to James of Scotland was made clear in Holinshed's narrative, Banquo was a party to Macbeth's murder of Duncan, but not to the other murder – Duff by Donwald – the main model for the murder in the *Macbeth* play. So by mixing the chronicles the play protected Banquo's image.

In Kit Marlowe's *Edward II*, Queen Isabella, though not a designing woman in the mould of Queen Catherine, Alice Arden and Lady Macbeth, nevertheless was the main inciter of the younger Mortimer to oppose Edward, ostensibly because of Edward's infatuation with Gaveston. She will fall back on Mortimer, but hopes this may not be necessary if Mortimer performs the service of removing Gaveston. Isabella appears to have arranged matters so that she cannot lose, but fate catches up with her from an unexpected source. Her son eventually disowns her.

What was the reason for this suspicion of designing women which 'divine Zenocrate' in *Tamburlaine* and Abigail in *The Jew of Malta* did not foreshadow. Did Tom Watson's wife, a member of the Swift family who had quarrelled with Bradley, have a larger part in Tom Watson's involvement with the affray than is recorded? Did Kit blame her?

Even Joan of Arc in *Henry VI*, Part One, a later version of *Harry VI* with which Marlowe had been involved, was less sympathetic in the play than in Holinshed's chronicle. Joan is treated with Marlovean irony, and foreshadows *Doctor Faustus* when she calls on evil spirits. After she is captured by the English, she says:

A plaguing mischief light on Charles and thee!

1 The north prospect of Canterbury in the seventeenth century showing how the Cathedral, adjoined by King's School, dominated the landscape

2 The school room in which Marlowe studied, as it was in his time (except for the clock)

INGS SCHOOL CANTERBURY.

3 The North Gate which Kit Marlowe passed each day on the way from hi
father's shop to King's School

4 The 'dark entry' mentioned in *The Jew of Malta*, with the
Cathedral towering behind, as in Marlowe's time

5 St Benet's church-
yard Cambridge over-
looked by the old part of
Corpus Christi. This
is much the same as
the view Marlowe
would have known

6 The Eagle public house opposite Corpus Christi with its restored
playactors' gallery. Students in Marlowe's time watched plays in this
courtyard

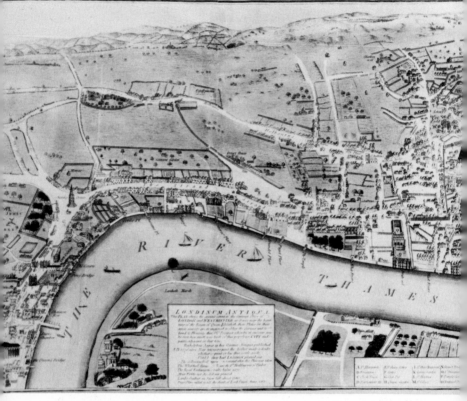

7 London in Marlowe's time. The theatres were built outside the city walls which are clearly marked

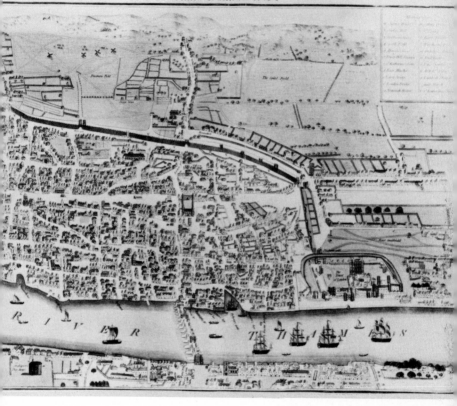

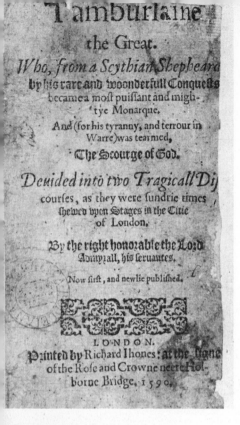

8 The title page of the first edition of *Tamburlaine the Great*, printed by Richard Jones in 1590. Marlowe's name is not mentioned but the Lord Admiral's players are, and the Scourge of God theme is stated

9 The 1598 edition of *Edward II* in which the characters of the court favourite Piers Gaveston and Edward I are given equal importance

10 Edward Alleyn who played
the leading roles in *Tamburlaine*,
The Jew of Malta, *The Massacre
at Paris* and *Dr Faustus*

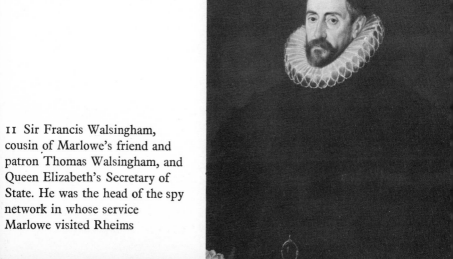

11 Sir Francis Walsingham,
cousin of Marlowe's friend and
patron Thomas Walsingham, and
Queen Elizabeth's Secretary of
State. He was the head of the spy
network in whose service
Marlowe visited Rheims

12 Sir Walter Raleigh, founder of the 'School of Night'

13 Marlowe's signature on the will of Mistress Katherine Benchkin. The others are those of his father, his uncle and his brother-in-law

> And may ye both be suddenly surpris'd
> By bloody hands, in sleeping on your beds!

This seems to refer to Macbeth in 'bloody hands' and 'sleeping on your beds'. The play of *Henry VI* was earlier than Shakespeare's *Macbeth*, but as both stories were in Holinshed's chronicles, they could have been read simultaneously.

It must be noted that when Kit Marlowe wrote the latter part of *Doctor Faustus*, and *Hero and Leander*, the theme of evil designing women had ceased to matter to him. Helen, from *Doctor Faustus*, is called the most majestic woman in the world. On her second appearance peerless verse is written about her.

> Was this the face that launched a thousand ships,
> And burnt the topless towers of Ilium?
> Sweet Helen, make me immortal with a kiss.
> Her lips suck forth my soul: see where it flies.
> Come, Helen, come, give me my soul again.
> Here will I dwell, for heaven is in those lips,
> And all is dross that is not Helena.
> I will be Paris, and for love of thee
> Instead of Troy shall Wittenberg be sacked,
> And I will combat with weak Menelaus,
> And wear thy colours on my plumed crest.
> Yea, I will wound Achilles in the heel,
> And then return to Helen for a kiss.
> Oh, thou art fairer than the evening's air,
> Clad in the beauty of a thousand stars.
> Brighter art thou than flaming Jupiter,
> When he appeared to hapless Semele:
> More lovely than the monarch of the sky,
> In wanton Arethusa's azure arms,
> And none but thou shalt be my paramour.
>
> (Act 5)

Helen did not save Faustus, but she was not the cause of his downfall.

In *Hero and Leander* it is the man, Leander, who is responsible for Hero's downfall. She is an innocent, chaste girl, 'Venus' Nun'. Leander is so beautiful that both sexes would be attracted to him, but it is Hero whom he loves.

> And in the midst a silver altar stood;
> There Hero sacrificing turtles' blood,
> Vailed to the ground, vailing her eyelids close,
> And modestly they opened as she rose:
> Thence flew Love's arrow with the golden head,
> And thus Leander was enamouréd.
> Stone still he stood, and evermore he gazed . . .
> It lies not in our power to love or hate,
> For will in us is overruled by fate . . .
> Where both deliberate, the love is slight;
> Who ever loved, that loved not at first sight?

Parts of this long poem have a dry wit, and give a tongue-in-cheek impression:

> There might you see the gods in sundry shapes,
> Committing heady riots, incest, rapes . . .
> Jove slyly stealing from his sister's bed
> To dally with Idalian Ganymede,
> Or for his love Europa bellowing loud,
> Or tumbling with the Rainbow in a cloud;
> Blood-quaffing Mars, heaving the iron net . . .

But there is none of the bitterness, or even the cutting irony, of *The Jew, The Massacre, Edward II*, or *Arden* or *Harry VI*.

The love-making is handled tastefully, with sympathy for innocent Hero.

> The nearer that he came, the more she fled,
> And seeking refuge, slipped into her bed.
> Whereon Leander sitting thus began,
> Through numbing cold, all feeble, faint and wan:

'If not for love, yet, love, for pity's sake,
Me in thy bed and maiden bosom take'...
Herewith affrighted Hero shrunk away,
And in her lukewarm place Leander lay...
Wherein Leander on her quivering breast
Breathless spoke something, and sighed out the rest;
Which so prevailed, as he with small ado
Enclosed her in his arms and kissed her too.
And every kiss to her as was a charm,
And to Leander as a fresh alarm,
So that the truce was broke, and she alas
(Poor silly maiden) at his mercy was.

The poem continues in this vein, and being unfinished at the time of the Deptford incident, remained unfinished until George Chapman (who translated Homer) completed it and dedicated his section to Thomas Walsingham's wife. Marlowe's section was dedicated to Thomas Walsingham by the printer Edward Blout.

So by 1593 Kit Marlowe could write with sympathy of Hero, as he did of Zenocrate and Abigail before the Hog Lane sword fight.

As well as disillusion with Tom Watson's wife, Kit himself had, during his early life in Canterbury, experienced disagreeable sisters. The 'cursing' Joan of *Henry VI* sounds like his sister who was accused of blasphemy in Canterbury – just as Abigail may have represented his gentle sister Margaret.

Speculation has also connected Kit Marlowe with Audrey Shelton, who was eventually to marry Thomas Walsingham.

10 · 1590

Kit Marlowe's play *The Jew of Malta* had become an established favourite and was drawing large audiences when the records of Philip Henslowe's Rose Theatre began in 1591–2. Before Henslowe's diary there were local records of where some of the acting companies visited, including Marlowe's Lord Admiral's Players, and though these lists do not give the names of the dramas presented, they are some guide to the activities of the companies with which Kit operated; and as only Henslowe's records of a single London theatre have survived, local records such as they are, are the only guide to the companies which did not come within Henslowe's orbit.

Two early mentions of performances by the Lord Admiral's company are from court records of 1588–9. The Lord Admiral's company presumably was chosen to perform at court because its patron had successfully led the defence against the Spanish Armada a few months earlier. Marlowe's *The Massacre at Paris* was probably prepared for one of these occasions, with its actual mention of the Armada, 'the king of Spain's huge fleet', and patriotic and topical references. As Kit Marlowe was the troupe's leading playwright with first-hand knowledge of France, and the Guise gave Ned Alleyn a choice part with which to entertain the court, it would have been apt.

At the end of 1589, when public playing was forbidden in the city of London, the Lord Admiral's company acquired merit by obeying the edict, while Lord Strange's company did not, as is seen from a letter written by the Lord Mayor to Lord Burleigh.

My very honourable good L. Where by a letter of your Lps. directed to m^r Yonge it appered vnto me, that it was your honours pleasure I sholde geue order for the staie of all playes within the Cittie, in that m^r Tilney did vtterly mislike the same. According to which your Lps. good pleasure, I presentlye sente for suche players as I coulde here of, so as there appered yesterday before me the L. Admeralles and the L. Straunges players, to whome I speciallie gaue in Charge and required them in her Maiesties name to forbere playinge, vntill further order mighte be geuen for theire allowance in that repecte: Where-upon the L. Admeralles players very dutifullie obeyed, but the others in very Contemptuous manner departing from me, went to the Crosse keys and played that afternoon, to the greate offence of the better sorte that knewe they were prohibited by order from your L. Which as I might not suffer, so I sent for the said Contemptuous persons, who haueing no reason to alleadge for theire Contempt, I coulde do no lesse but this evening Comitt some of them to one of the Compters, and do meane according to your Lps. direction to prohibite all playing, vntill your Lps. pleasure therein be further knowen. And thus resting further to trouble your L., I moste humblie take my leaue. At London the Sixte of Nouember 1589.

The Lord Admiral's players were to merge with Lord Strange's company, and it was to be this troupe which appeared frequently from 1591 onwards at the Rose Theatre, production details of which were recorded by Philip Henslowe.

Among the surviving provincial accounts of the period are records of visits by the Lord Admiral's Men in 1589–90 to Ipswich, Maidstone, Winchester, Marlborough, Gloucester, Coventry and Oxford. In 1590–91 they appeared with the Earl of Sussex's players and the Queen's players at Southampton on Shrove Sunday (14 February); at Winchester 'by order of the mayor this year'; at Bath, with 'my L. Stranges plaiers'; at Gloucester, again with 'the Queenes and the Earle of Sussex players'; and at Oxford.

The merged company with Lord Strange's players appeared at court (Whitehall) 'for six severall plays' on 27 and 28 December, 1 and 9 January and 6 and 8 February in the 1591–2 period. The

Earle of Sussex's Men appeared once, on 2 January, the only other troupe mentioned in the court records at this time.

Another group still called the Admiral's Players was to continue touring in the provinces, and Lord Strange's merged company also toured. They were in Canterbury in July 1592 when 'they played in the courte hall before Mr Lawes maior & other his brethren',* for which they received thirty shillings. This was an occasion when Kit Marlowe may have been present and *The Jew of Malta* may have been performed. The pride of the Marlowe family in these circumstances can be imagined! This would also account for some of the play's Canterbury references.

The first record of a performance by the Earl of Pembroke's players, for whom Kit Marlowe was to write *Edward II,* was at Christmas 1592, when they shared court appearances with Lord Strange's troupe at Hampton Court. 'December 26; January 6. the servantes of the Erle of Pembroke. December 27, 31, January 1. the Servantes of the Lorde Strange.'

Edward Alleyn returned to the Lord Admiral's patronage; by the plague time of 1593 he was described as 'Edward Allen, servaunt to the right honourable the Lord Highe Admiral', while 'William Kemp, Thomas Pope, John Heminges, Augustine Phillipes and Georg Brian' were 'al one companie, servauntes to our verie good Lord the Lord Strainge' in a Privy Council warrant. Kit Marlowe was to leave Pembroke's Men to finish *Doctor Faustus* for Edward Alleyn to perform.

In the first season at the Rose, as presented by the merged company of Lord Strange with the Admiral's Men, *The Jew of Malta* and '*Harey the vj*' featured prominently, and by May 1592 the *Tamburlaines* had joined the repertoire. Another prominent play was Thomas Kyd's '*Jeronymo*'.

Kit Marlowe became involved with Thomas Kyd sometime after he was released from Newgate prison while Thomas Watson stayed behind. Thomas Kyd was, with Kit Marlowe, the other

---

* Mr. Leeds was in fact the mayor.

great playwright of the beginning of the theatres. It was inevitable that they should meet, though they had little in common other than their profession of playwright, and in their writing for a time for the same company.

Thomas Kyd was born in London and baptized on 6 November 1558, more than five years earlier than Kit Marlowe and William Shakespeare. He was the son of a scrivener and was educated at Merchant Taylor's School under Richard Mulcaster, as was Edmund Spenser. He did not, like Spenser and Marlowe, move on to Cambridge and like Shakespeare did not attend university, but nevertheless received a good education at school. He was not empathetic and adaptable as Shakespeare became, and did not pick up information later as Shakespeare did, hence his history, geography, French, Latin and Italian were suspect. He was not a great poet, but his dramatic structure was good and he was the father of the revenge play, which later became part of Elizabethan 'tragedy'.

Thomas Kyd followed his father's profession for a time. A scrivener was a drafter of documents, a notary, and such training in the construction of written documents provided the background for his contribution to the growth of drama by his example of good construction. Until *The Jew of Malta* and *Edward II*, Marlowe's plays did not equal Kyd's in structure, though they were superior in poetry and *élan*. Kyd's masterpiece was *The Spanish Tragedy*.

Kyd's other great play was the first part of *Heironimo* (or *Jeronymo*) to which *The Spanish Tragedy* was in some ways a sequel. This shows the popularity of Kyd's play. In Kyd's case, *The Spanish Tragedy* is considered the better work.

The earlier play about Hieronimo dealt with honour, in war and peace, and in *The Spanish Tragedy*, the coming of dishonour brought the need for revenge, making it the first great revenge play and the precursor of Elizabethan 'tragedy'.

As *The Spanish Tragedy* was performed simultaneously with Marlowe's plays, neither Kyd nor Marlowe influenced each other, except in the inclusion of exciting bloodshed and blank verse. Shakespeare's *Hamlet* was to be the greatest of all revenge plays, and it would be interesting to compare his play with Kyd's lost *Hamlet*. Shakespeare's *Hamlet* also has many Marlowe references, including, from Hamlet's soliloquy,

> But that the dread of something after death,
> The undiscover'd country from whose bourn
> No traveller returns . . .

which echoes Mortimer's speech from Marlowe's *Edward II*:

> Farewell, fair queen; weep not for Mortimer
> That scorns the world, and as a traveller
> Goes to discover countries yet unknown.

Kit Marlowe's ex-friend from Cambridge, Thomas Nashe, in a preface to Greene's *Menaphon* (1589) entitled 'To the Gentlemen Students', attacked Thomas Kyd. He first referred to Kyd by his previous trade as a scrivener and notary (a 'Noverint'), then to his sub-Senecan type of drama, singling out *Hamlet,* and followed with a pun about Kid in Aesop. It began bitingly:

It is a common practise now a dayes amongst a sort of shifting companions, that runne through every Art and thrive by none, to leave the trade of Noverint, whereto they were borne, and busie themselves with the indevours of Art, that could scarcely Latinize their neck verse if they shoulde have neede; yet English Seneca by Candlelight yeelds many good sentences . . . and if you intreate him faire in a frostie morning, hee will afford you whole Hamlets . . . The Sea exhaled by droppes will in continuance bee drie, and Seneca, let blood line by line and page by page, at length must needes die to our Stage; which makes his famished followers to imitate the Kid in Æsop, who, enamoured with the Foxes new fangles, forsooke all hopes of life to leape into his new occupation . . .

One place where Kit Marlowe saw playwrights like Thomas Kyd was St Paul's Churchyard, where many printers and booksellers had stalls, complete with hanging signs, near the walls;

but Kyd, in his letter to Sir John Puckering (1593), did not own to meeting there himself.

... for more assurance that I was not of that vile opinion, Lett it but please yor Lp to enquire of such as he [Marlowe] conversed wth all, that is (as I am geven to vnderstand) wth Harriott, Warner, Royden, and some stationers in Paules churchyard, whom I in no sort can accuse nor will excuse by reson of his companie ...

Thomas Watson came out of prison on 12 February 1590. He celebrated his release by publishing a book of Italian madrigals with the composer William Byrd. These were 'Italian Madrigalls Englished, not to the sense of the original dittie, but after the affection of the Noate by Thomas Watson, Gentleman. There are also heere inferred two excellent Madrigalls of Master William Byrds, composed after the Italian vaine, at the request of the said Thomas Watson.'

Kit Marlowe had made some new contacts during his friend's absence, but he would nevertheless have welcomed Tom Watson's return.

In 1590 Sir Francis Walsingham died. He had been one of England's most loyal servants, a staunch supporter of Protestant Queen Elizabeth, and remarkable for having set up the first English spy service. From his period as ambassador in Paris at the time of the Massacre of St Bartholomew (which gave the title to Kit Marlowe's *The Massacre at Paris*) he had been aware of the desire of militant Catholics to defeat Protestantism, and had urged Elizabeth to recognize the danger this meant to her. He saw supporters of the Catholic Mary Queen of Scots as part of this larger danger, and had been instrumental in securing her downfall. Sir Francis, because he knew Spain would attack England, used his spy network to amass news of the Armada's preparation and it was as part of this that Kit Marlowe acted when he visited Rheims from Cambridge in the pre-Armada period. Through his spy work Kit met his lifelong patron Thomas Walsingham, a younger cousin of Sir Francis. Sir Francis's only child

Frances married Sir Philip Sidney, the chivalric ideal who died a legendary death in 1586 (and left his father-in-law to pay his debts), and later married the Earl of Essex, who was to rebel abortively at the end of his career; but this rebellion was a long time after her father's death.

The payment of Sir Philip Sidney's debts, and lack of financial recompense from the queen he had served so loyally, had left Sir Francis Walsingham deep in debt, and he remained so until he died. In court circles, Elizabeth can hardly have gained in popularity by her miserly treatment of Sir Francis. Nevertheless, in the post-Armada scare of 1598, Thomas Walsingham (with Sir Thomas Leveson) assumed command of the defence system of the Medway, which his cousin had set up ten years before, and the family's tradition of loyalty continued.

Thomas Watson wrote a memorial poem after Sir Francis's death, called 'Meliboeus'. In it Corydon (Thomas Watson) and Tityrus (Thomas Walsingham) mourned the death of Meliboeus (Sir Francis Walsingham). Watson, who had received considerable patronage from the Walsingham family, had reason to mourn Sir Francis's passing as well as to maintain his association with the family by enshrining his grief in verse. The English version of 'Meliboeus' – the original was in Latin – was dedicated to Sir Francis's daughter Frances, Lady Sidney as she then was.

The death of Sir Francis Walsingham altered the balance of power among Elizabeth's advisers and left the Cecils still more powerful, which did not help Thomas Walsingham's protégés such as Kit Marlowe.

Thomas Walsingham was later to improve his standing by marrying Audrey Shelton, who was related to Queen Elizabeth through the Boleyns. Audrey was to become a Lady of Her Majesty's Bed-chamber, and was to maintain her position at court when James ascended the throne. Queen Elizabeth visited Scadbury in 1597, and may have knighted Thomas then, and Thomas also received the manors of Dartford, Cobham, Combe and Chislehurst in 1597, so he was in high favour. (The first known reference to Audrey as Lady Walsingham was in Chapman's dedication to her of his completion of Kit Marlowe's *Hero and Leander*.) But he was temporarily less powerful in 1590.

Frances Walsingham, as Lady Sidney, and later, though with less affection from Queen Elizabeth, as the Countess of Essex, always maintained standing in court. But once Sir Francis was dead, Lord Burleigh and his son Robert Cecil were in an unassailable position. Audrey is said to have become a favourite with Robert Cecil later, but the immediate result of the death of Sir Francis Walsingham was the removal from Walsingham family protégés like Kit Marlowe and Tom Watson of the undeniable strength of the backing of Sir Francis. Had Sir Francis been available to help in 1593, when Marlowe was accused of atheism as he had been in 1587 over the Rheims visit, the result might have been different.

1590 was a fateful year for Kit Marlowe. He had yet to complete his best works – *Edward II*, *Doctor Faustus* and *Hero and Leander*. But his most valuable backer, Sir Francis Walsingham, had died; and his activities had become diffuse due partly to the absence at the beginning of 1590 of his mentor Thomas Watson. One positive milestone had been achieved – the two *Tamburlaines* were published in 1590 and they survive for posterity as Kit Marlowe edited them.

11 · The Playwrights' Brains Trust

Dido, Queen of Carthage, written by Kit Marlowe and Thomas Nashe in their student days at Cambridge, was 'played by the children of her Majesty's Chapel' and was published the year after the Deptford tragedy, 1594. As this play was mainly a translation from Virgil's *Aeneid* it did not grace the stage as naturally as Marlowe's other dramas, and belongs with Marlowe's translations (Ovid and Lucan). It is interesting because it was a collaboration in dramatic form. The action from Act II, Scene i, of this play appears in the first players' scene in Shakespeare's *Hamlet,* and is mentioned in *The Tempest.* So Shakespeare had seen or read Marlowe's and Nashe's play in one form or another. Playwrights, including Marlowe and Shakespeare, began writing some 'royal historical' plays as collaborations about 1591–2, and these, apart from *Harry VI,* were performed by Pembroke's Men.

This was a period of fluidity between the companies, and it is interesting to list what the merged Admiral's/Strange's company was performing at the Rose. The plays included Kit Marlowe's *The Jew of Malta, Tamburlaine, The Massacre at Paris* (known as 'the tragedy of the Guyes' after the murdering Duke of Guise), *Harry VI* and *Titus* which could refer to the earlier *Titus and Vespacia* or might mean *Titus Andronicus* and lend weight to the theory that Kyd (whose *Jeronymos* were performed by this company) or Peele did pre-Shakespeare work on the play. At the beginning of 1594 at the Rose, the Earl of Sussex's Men, who staged *The Jew of Malta,* also performed *Titus and Ondronicus,* which certainly refers to *Titus Andronicus.* In the earlier 1592 list at the Rose, 'the taner of Denmarke' was staged on 23 May, which might bear relationship with *Hamlet*, sub-titled 'The Prince of Denmark'.

When playwright Robert Greene was dying in September 1592 and repenting his profligate life, in his *Groatsworth of Wit* he warned fellow playwrights Kit Marlowe, George Peele and Thomas Nashe to beware of similar fates. He described one of the 'evils' as 'an upstart crow, beautified with our feathers' with his 'Tygers hart wrapt in a Players hyde', a 'Johannes factotum' who considered himself the 'only Shakes-scene in the country'. This is usually thought to be Shakespeare. If this is the first written reference to Shakespeare, the implication was that an actor and jack-of-all-trades had turned to writing plays in which he plagiarized the works of real playwrights. The quotation, altered in one word – '*player's* hide' had been substituted for '*woman's* hide' – came from *Henry VI*, Part Three, which resembles an earlier play, *The True Tragedy of Richard Duke of York*, that might have work by Marlowe and others in it – though *Henry VI*, Part Three, does seem like all Shakespeare, while *Titus Andronicus* does not. *The True Tragedy* was performed by Pembroke's Men, for whom Marlowe, alone, wrote *Edward II*. The first written reference to Shakespeare as 'a player' was at Christmas 1594, when he appeared at court as one of the Lord Chamberlain's company, but he was in London in 1593 when *Venus and Adonis* was written, and could have been indulging his various talents there in 1592.

During the 1590–91 period Kit Marlowe had begun sharing a room with Thomas Kyd, presumably after the merger of the Admiral's Men with Lord Strange's company. It is a mystery why he and Marlowe came to share, unless it was convenience because they were both working for the merged company; they were unlike as people and had little in common except their profession. Peele, and even Greene, were more likely collaborators with Marlowe for *Harry VI*, and Peele may also have worked with Kyd on *Titus Andronicus*. *Arden of Faversham* was published anonymously by the printer responsible for Kyd's plays, but it is more likely that this was a draft by Marlowe which became mixed with Kyd's papers (as Kyd later claimed had happened with an heretical draft) than that he and Marlowe worked on it together, as there is little of Kyd's style in this play but plenty of Marlowe's.

Did the newcomer Shakespeare join this Brains Trust of play-wrights? The 'Johannes factotum' sounds an outsider, though Chettle later apologized to him on dead Greene's behalf, and Shakespeare's references to Marlowe were always of the warmest.

Nashe's attack on Kyd in 'To the Gentlemen Students' was in the same vein as Greene's criticism of the 'Johannes factotum', which sounds like snobbery of the graduate playwrights against the others. Kyd's resentment of this might have continued against graduate Marlowe, though Marlowe was not responsible for the jibe.

George Peele, an Oxford graduate, who was like Watson in age and in being a jester, was the one warned most against plagiarists in Greene's *Groatsworth of Wit*:

. . . and thou, no less deserving than the other two, in some things rarer, in nothing inferior – driven as myself to extreme shifts, a little I have to say to thee; and, were it not an idolatrous oath, I would swear by sweet St George [a pun on Peele's Christian name] thou art unworthy better hap, since thou dependest on so mean a stay. Base-minded men all three of you, if by my misery ye be not warned: for unto none of you, like me, sought those butts to cleave – those puppets, I mean, that speak from our mouths [actors], those antics garnished in our colours. Is it not strange that I, to whom they all have been beholden, is it not like that you, to whom they all have been beholden, shall – were ye in that case that I am now – be both at once of them forsaken.

Greene, dying in penury, was forsaken by the actors who were fair-weather friends. Marlowe, Nashe and Peele should take heed. The Shake-scene *was* an actor.

Greene said to Marlowe:

Wonder not (for with thee will I first begin) thou famous gracer of tragedians [an acknowledgement of Marlowe's status in the theatrical world] that Greene, who hath said with thee (like the fool in his heart) 'There is no God', should now give glory unto his greatness: for penetrating is his power, his hand lyes heavie upon me, hee hath spoken unto mee with a voice of thunder, and I have felt he is a God that can punish enemies. Why should thy excellent wit, his gift, bee so blinded, that thou shouldst give no glorie to the giver: Is it pestilent Machiavellian pollicy that thou hast studied? O peevish follie! ... and wilt thou, my friend, be his disciple? Look unto me, by him persuaded to that liberty, and thou shalt find it an infernal bondage. I know the least of my demerits merit this miserable death, but wilful striving against known truth, exceedeth all the terrors of my soul.

Kit remembered this when he was writing the last part of *Doctor Faustus.*

> O, if my soul must suffer for my sin,
> Impose some end to my incessant pain!

> Stand still, you ever-moving spheres of Heaven
> That time may cease and midnight never come!
>
> (Marlowe)

Defer not, with me, till this last point of extremity; for little knowest thou how in the end thou shalt be visited. (Greene)

Greene mentioned other sins to all his dramatist friends:

Delight not, as I have done, in irreligious oaths; for, from the blasphemer's house, a curse shall not depart. Despise drunkenness, which wasteth wit, and maketh men all equal to the beasts. Fly lust, as the deathman of the soul, and defile not the temple of the Holy Ghost. Abhor those epicures, whose loose life hath made religion loathsome to your ears; and when they soothe you with terms of Mastership, remember Robert Greene, whom they have so often flattered, perishes now for want of comfort.

Did this suggest the parade of the seven deadly sins in *Doctor Faustus* to Marlowe?'

Shakespeare, though less impressed by Greene, was much impressed with *Doctor Faustus*, to which he frequently referred in his philosophical play *The Tempest* some years later.

To Nashe, Greene advised against too much bitter pamphleteering: 'young Juvenal, that biting satirist, that lastly with me together writ a comedy. Sweet boy, might I advise thee, be advised and get not many enemies by bitter words: inveigh against vain men, for thou canst do it, no man better, no man so well . . . Then blame not scholars vexed with sharp lines, if they reprove thy too much liberty of reproof.'

Greene did as much harm to Kit Marlowe's reputation, for all his friendly warnings, as Kyd was to achieve when he informed on Marlowe. It was Greene who misinterpreted the 'daring Mohamet' scene in *Tamburlaine* into 'daring God from heaven', and labelled *Tamburlaine* 'atheist'. As early as 1588, the year after the great success of the two *Tamburlaines*, he wrote in the letter 'To the Gentlemen Readers' in *Perimedes the Blacke-Smith*:

I keepe my old course, to palter up something in Prose, using mine old poesie still . . . for that I could not make my verses yet upon the stage in tragicall buskins, everie word filling the mouth like the faburden of Bo-Bell, daring God out of heaven with that Atheist 'Tamburlan' or blaspheming with the mad preest of the sonne: but let me rather pocket up the Asse of Diogenes: than wantonlye set out such impious instances of intollerable poetrie: such mad and scoffing poets, that have propheticall spirits, as bred of Merlin's race . . .

The label of atheist thus attached to Kit Marlowe by Greene was taken up by Kyd in 1593 to explain how he came to have the heretical paper: '. . . some fragments of a disputation toching that opinion, affirmed by Marlowe to be his, and shufled wth some of myne unknown to me . . .' Kyd continued: 'That I should love or be familiar frend wth one so irreligious, were verie rare . . . besides he was intemp(er)ate & of a cruel hart, the verie contraries to wch my greatest enemies will saie about me.'

Most comments by others about Kit Marlowe were complimentary and even affectionate, and John Marston said the opposite of Kyd's 'cruel hart' jibe, referring to 'kinde Kit Marlowe'. Few comments of any sort survive about Thomas Kyd.

When Kyd spoke of 'writinge in one chamber twoe years synce' he meant precisely what he said – his other profession of scrivener and notary had made him aware of the meaning of words. This has been wrongly interpreted by some to mean that Kit Marlowe and Thomas Kyd set up house together. Writing in one chamber would be rather like sharing an office, and is a concrete example of how Elizabethan playwrights worked together, though Marlowe and Kyd were an odd combination. The seeds of both their personal tragedies may have been sown by two such different people working together.

A similar wrong derivation has turned Eleanor Bull's house in Deptford, where the brawl was to take place in 1593, into a tavern, when at no stage was it ever thus described in the original document.

As the playwrights began to cooperate in 1590–91, the future of the growing theatrical profession looked exciting, if hazardous, and possibly glamorous. A permanent framework had been established by the legalization of the acting companies under patronage and the construction of theatres to house plays in London. Though the playwrights did not get sufficient or regular reward, they did have an opportunity to make playwriting their main profession if there was subsidy from elsewhere. It was a natural step that they should join together into a kind of 'union', though the nature of their profession made them likely to have internal feuds. Kit Marlowe may not have moved so deeply into this company had Tom Watson not been detained for so long in Newgate prison, and Shakespeare certainly learned (from Marlowe?) not to become too involved.

Thomas Nashe, who once criticized Marlowe, was to return to his defence after Kit's death. He not only published their joint play the next year, thus publicizing his association with Marlowe, but he made several other friendly mentions. In *Lenten Stuffe* in 1599 he wrote a parody of Kit's *Hero and Leander* and also said:

Let me see, hath any bodie in Yarmouth heard of Leander and Hero, of whome divine Musaeus sung, and a diviner muse than him, Kit Marlow. Two faithfull lovers they were, as every apprentise in Paules Churchyard will tell you for your love, and sel you for your mony . . .

To Thomas Thorpe, who was to publish Marlowe's translation of Lucan in 1600, Kit was 'a pure elemental wit'.

In *Brief Lives* John Aubrey wrote that Ben Jonson 'killed Mr Marlow, the poet, on Bunhill, comeing from the Green Curtain playhouse'. This gives the impression that Kit Marlowe was respected as, if there was anything unpleasant to be found or alleged about a person, Aubrey always unearthed it. Ben Jonson did, in fact, kill an actor who was not, of course, Kit Marlowe.

So 1591 saw a recognizable group of playwrights associating together, and this was to continue. Opportunities in the theatrical profession were to increase in the next year when the Rose theatre was opened by Henslowe, and a new company – Pembroke's Men – came into prominence along with the continued merger between the troupes of the Lord Admiral and Lord Strange. Plays by Marlowe were performed by all these companies, so his play writing career was very successful at this stage.

12 . Piers Gaveston

In 1592 a Jesuit conspirator against the Queen was heard to suggest that Lord Burleigh (Cecil) had power 'far more noysome and pernitious to the realme' than that of Gaveston at Edward II's court (dramatized in Kit Marlowe's play). This Jesuit was Robert Parsons, who also spoke against Walter Raleigh's 'School of Atheism'. The informer against Kit Marlowe, Baines, was to write similarly in 1593 of 'Christofer Marley' who 'perswades men to Atheism willing them not to be afeard of bugbeares and hobgoblins and utterly scorning both god and ministers . . .'

Parsons and Baines both hoped to discredit English Protestants; though Marlowe was only a protégé of the Walsinghams, they could be attacked through him, and Raleigh's 'School' had representatives in very high places. Of Kit Marlowe's first brush with Baines, which took place in Holland in January 1592, Sir Robert Sidney wrote to Lord Burleigh: 'The scholer [Marlowe] sais himself to be very wel known both to the Earle of Northumberland [a member of the School of Night] and my lord Strang [Lord Strange of the acting company]. Bains and he do also accuse one another of intent to goe to the Ennemy or to Rome, both as they say of malice one to another . . .'* So Baines was at this time not accusing Marlowe of atheism at all, but of the 1587 charge of 'going to Rome', of which the Privy Council cleared him at Corpus Christi college. Marlowe was *not* going to Rome, but *he* accused Baines of this. Both Jesuit Parsons's criticisms and those of Baines were meant to discredit Protestants by describing them

---

* This letter was recently discovered by R. B. Wernham, and printed in the April 1976 edition of the *English Historical Review*.

as atheists, or as papist plotters; in the case of Lord Burleigh, they attempted to discredit a powerful minister by saying he was only a court favourite and did not deserve power. It is a coincidence that the analogy used by Parsons against Burleigh was in fact taken from Marlowe's own play, though the Edward II story was to be written about by several others as well as Marlowe. Parsons and Baines were part of the movement to secure the throne for a Roman Catholic after Elizabeth's death, and the consequences of their actions affected Kit Marlowe considerably, as well as other prominent Protestants.

The incident in Flushing in January 1592, involving Kit Marlowe, Richard Baines, and a goldsmith named Gifford Gilbert, was a strange one. Gilbert 'uttered' a Dutch shilling made of 'plain peuter', with the intention, he claimed, of demonstrating to Marlowe and Baines how this could be done. Baines reported it to Sir Robert Sidney, and Marlowe and Gilbert were sent back to England in custody, but with a recommendation for mercy, as only one peuter Dutch shilling had been coined. This recommendation was accepted, and nothing happened to them.

Marlowe's play *Edward II*, dealing with Edward's infatuation with Gaveston, the opposition of the barons led by the younger Mortimer, and Mortimer's alliance with Edward's wife Isabella, was originally called: 'The Troublesome raigne and lamentable death of Edward the second, King of England: with the tragicall fall of proud Mortimer', but by the 1598 edition it was extended to include 'And also the life and death of Piers Gaveston, the greate Earle of Cornewall, and mighty favourite of king Edward the second, as it was publiquely acted by the right honourable the Earle of Pembrooke his servants'. So while the atheism charge by Catholic conspirators against Protestants remained an 'underground movement', the idea of 'court favourite' as a criticism caught the public imagination and strengthened. Marlowe, the victim of one criticism, inadvertently helped to promulgate another through his play.

Nevertheless, while the leading court figures were mainly

Protestant (Lord Strange was a Catholic loyal to Queen Elizabeth, who was to meet his death by poison after refusing to conspire against her) they did not all agree about who the Protestant successor to Queen Elizabeth should be. This is why the 'court favourite' criticism was so widespread, and was advanced by both Protestants and Catholics. Kit Marlowe had again caught the feeling of the times in one of his plays.

The relationship between Edward II and Gaveston was a homosexual one, but Parsons was not accusing Burleigh of homosexuality, only of holding power by the sovereign's favour rather than by ability or public choice. Drayton, who also wrote of the Edward II story a few years after Marlowe, stressed homosexuality more than Marlowe did:

> And in my place, upon his Regall Throne,
> To set that Girle-boy, wanton Gaveston.

And he noted 'the effeminacie and luxurious wantonness of Gaveston, the Kings Minion; his Behaviour and Attire ever so Woman-like, to please the Eye of his lascivious Master'.

When Marlowe is posthumously accused of homosexuality because he dramatized Piers Gaveston, it should be remembered that the source material (Holinshed and other chronicles) made this point, and so did other writers of the time, and they were not all homosexual because they chose to write about this story.

Homosexuality and a court favourite were not surprising partners because James VI of Scotland (later to be James I of England) in fact had a homosexual court favourite who was expelled by the nobles – his relative Esmé Stuart. This may be what led Marlowe, Drayton and the others to make Gaveston their example of a court favourite.

A court character who was more praiseworthy for his abilities, though a risk for monarchs to entertain, was Bolingbroke, as portrayed in Shakespeare's play *Richard II*, the 'partner' play to Marlowe's *Edward II*. Bolingbroke was usually taken to represent the Earl of Essex, and the play was in fact acted the night before

Essex's rebellion nine years later; but when a note was pinned on James of Scotland's door in 1592 warning him to beware of the fate of Richard II, he was merely being warned about the danger of encouraging court favourites.

Since 1584, when *Leicester's Commonwealth* had been published abroad, court favourites had been criticized in England, and the Earl of Leicester was the example in this case. He was associated with favourites who had ruined Edward II, Richard II and Henry VI – all to be the subject of plays by Marlowe or Shakespeare, as well as by other contemporary writers. This was part of the politics of the age, caused by Protestant Elizabeth of England having no heir, Protestant James of Scotland being the chief claimant, and the playwrights needing to be in tune with the times to survive financially.

Queen Elizabeth was aware that Shakespeare's Bolingbroke was being likened to the Earl of Essex, as is shown by a memorandum prepared by William Lambarde on 4 August 1601.

. . . so her Majestie fell upon the reign of King Richard II. saying, 'I am Richard II. know ye not that?'

W. L. 'Such a wicked imagination was determined and attempted by a most unkind Gent. the most adorned creature that ever your Majestie made.'

Her Majestie. 'He that will forget God, will also forget his benefactors; this tragedy was played 40^{tie} times in open streets and houses.'

. . . returning to Richard II. she demanded, 'Whether I had seen any true picture, or lively representation of his countenance and person?'

W. L. 'None but such as be in common hands.'

Her Majestie. 'The Lord Lumley, a lover of antiquities, discovered it fastened on the backside of a door of a base room; which he presented unto me, praying, with my good leave, that I might put it in order with the Ancestors and Successors; I will command Tho. Kneavet, Keeper of my House and Gallery at Westminster, to show it unto thee.'

Kit Marlowe's *Edward II*, by presenting the court favourite as a homosexual, thus associating him with Esmé Stuart (though

Robert Parsons likened him to Lord Burleigh), was less likely to have distressed the Queen. There were, however, many similarities between Marlowe's *Edward II* and Shakespeare's *Richard II*, Marlowe's play usually being considered the better work because of its deeper examination of the subject and stronger characterization.

Marlowe's *Edward II* begins with customary élan.

Gaveston (reading a letter):
>   'My father is deceas'd. Come, Gaveston,
>   And share the kingdom with thy dearest friend.'
>   Ah, words that make me surfeit with delight!
>   What greater bliss can hap to Gaveston
>   Than live and be the favourite of a king!

The theme of a king's favourite has instantly been introduced. Three poor men approach Gaveston, to whom he is not sympathetic.

>   These are not men for me.
>   I must have wanton poets, pleasant wits,
>   Musicians, that with touching of a string
>   May draw the pliant king which way I please:

Marlowe could be referring to James's court in this passage, and goes on:

>   Music and poetry is his delight;
>   Therefore I'll have Italian masques by night,
>   Sweet speeches, comedies and pleasing shows.

More ambivalent pursuits are suggested:

>   And in the day, when he shall walk abroad,
>   Like sylvan nymphs my pages shall be clad;
>   My men, like satyrs grazing on the lawns,
>   Shall with their goat-feet dance an antic hay;

However, the barons led by the younger Mortimer are soon

organizing opposition, and so is the King's wife Isabella, who eventually joins forces with Mortimer. Not for nothing was Isabella known in the history chronicles as the she-wolf of France. If any character deserves sympathy in this tragedy it is 'pliant' Edward, who is no match for the strong forces ranged around him. His son, Edward III, is able to revenge his father by disowning his mother, but Edward II cannot cope with Gaveston, Isabella, Mortimer, or even with his lesser adherents Spenser and Baldock.

Edward II shows Marlowe coming of age as a dramatist. Twenty-three years of history are compressed into a swift narrative sequence. He cannot make a part for Alleyn in the story – Edward, Gaveston and Mortimer all impinge on each other – so the play is given to another company, Pembroke's Men, who must have been delighted with it – a new company receiving a play from London's leading playwright.

Though less bombastic than his earlier works, this play nevertheless has some marvellous speeches. Young Spenser's advice to Baldock on how to be a successful courtier is a masterpiece of irony.

> Then, Baldock, you must cast the scholar off,
> And learn to court it like a gentleman.
> 'Tis not a black cloak, fac'd before with serge,
> And smelling to a nosegay all the day,
> Or holding of a napkin in your hand,
> Or saying a long grace at table's end,
> Or making low legs to a nobleman
> Or looking downward, with your eyelids close,
> And saying, 'Truly, an't may please your honour,'
> Can get you any favour with great men.
> You must be proud, bold, pleasant, resolute,
> And now and then stab, as occasion serves.

Mortimer's farewell speech, which is echoed by Shakespeare in *Hamlet*, brings Walter Raleigh's changing fortunes to mind.

> Base Fortune, now I see, that in thy wheel
> There is a point, to which when men aspire,
> They tumble headlong down: that point I touch'd,
> And I, seeing there was no place to mount up higher,
> Why shall I grieve at my declining fall?
> Farewell, fair queen. Weep not for Mortimer,
> That scorns the world, and, as a traveller,
> Goes to discover countries yet unknown.

Edward's executioner Lightborn is a variant of Lucifer, of which his name is a partial translation. This links Marlowe's play with Dante's *Inferno*, his own *Doctor Faustus* and with Robert Greene's dire warning though it is not without black humour in the manner of *The Jew of Malta*.

> 'Tis not the first time I have killed a man.
> I learned in Naples how to poison flowers,
> To strangle with a lawn thrust through the throat,
> To pierce the windpipe with a needle's point;
> Or, whilst one is asleep, to take a quill
> And blow a little powder in his ears,
> Or open his mouth and pour quicksilver down.

The Jew of Malta poisoned flowers, and the latter part of the speech inspired Shakespeare to the way old Hamlet was killed by his brother.

Drayton, who was also to write about the Edward II theme, wrote a splendid piece about Kit Marlowe himself:

> Neat Marlowe, bathed in the Thespian springs,
> Had in him those brave translunary things
> That the first poets had; his raptures were
> All ayre and fire, which made his verses cleere;
> For that fine madness still he did retaine,
> Which rightly should possesse a poet's braine.

'Neat' in this context means 'natural, unsophisticated', which is an interesting description of Marlowe, sounding like the boy from Canterbury.

From a student with wide-ranging tastes, Kit Marlowe had become a man who noticed trends in life around him. An outgoing person, he was not a selfish one, nor was he egocentric. He did not attack other people, though several (especially Greene and Kyd) attacked him. And while he was a great talker in company about the new learning and how this affected religion, he was not forthcoming on his personal affairs. He had close friends – Thomas Watson, Thomas Walsingham, Thomas Hariot, at Cambridge Thomas Lewgar, and various others, but his plays are more about the characters he observed than himself. He had the courage of his convictions in following his own line of thought, and if hearsay comments can be believed, he was inclined to stir discussion by overstating. He had a sense of humour, though this was ironic, and sometimes sardonic, compared to the 'ready wit' of Nashe and Shakespeare's comedies. If he was often in the company of talking groups he must have been invited. The denigration begun by Greene, and continued by political opponents of Protestants like Baines, has obscured his character. He was a good friend and a pleasant if disturbing person to know. He was also well attuned to understanding the times, as his play *Edward II* shows.

13 · Visit to Canterbury

On 9 May 1592 Kit Marlowe appeared before Sir Owen Hopton, JP for Middlesex, and was bound over in the sum of £20 to attend the Michaelmas Assizes; he was to keep the peace towards Allen Nicholls, constable of Holywell Street, and Nicholas Helliott, under-constable. Holywell Street was in the theatrical area, as James Burbage had built the Theatre on grounds once belonging to the dissolved priory of Holywell and the street still bore its name.

Small fracas like the one in which Kit Marlowe was involved were fairly usual and no harm came to him. Also, in this case of 1592 he was referred to as 'Christopher Marle of London, gentleman', while he had been 'yoman' two years before in the Newgate affair. Shakespeare was involved in a similar dispute in November 1596, when William Wayte, stepson of a Surrey magistrate, William Gardiner, claimed that Francis Langley, who had bought the Paris Garden at Bankside to build a theatre, with William Shakespeare, Dorothy Soer and Anne Lee, threatened his life. Wayte took out 'sureties of the peace ... for fear of death and so forth'. The foursome must have prevailed as the Swan was built on this garden, though Langley ran into trouble later and Shakespeare, who had lived in the parish of St Helens, Bishopsgate, moved across the river leaving behind an unpaid due of five shillings.

Nevertheless, the incident in Holywell Street foreshadowed the disaster of the following year. More people than Marlowe would have been involved with these two constables.

After having been for some months without Tom Watson's companionship, Kit Marlowe was more likely to fall into such situations and Walsingham family protégés were less protected since the death of their most powerful member, Sir Francis, in 1590.

The repercussions of Sir Francis's death were still felt at court, as Queen Elizabeth had not yet filled his post of Secretary, and was not to do so for six years. The two immediate results were that Lord Burleigh fell to ploys, such as staging politically motivated plays, to persuade the Queen to appoint his son to this post, and the Earl of Essex, who was married to Sir Francis's daughter, had his ambitions increased because the position was unfilled. Shakespeare's portrait of Polonius in *Hamlet* describes Burleigh's habit at this time of imparting wise maxims to his son. For example: 'Be sure to keep some great man thy friend, but trouble him not with trifles . . . Towards thy superiors be humble, yet generous. With thine equals familiar, and yet respective. Towards thine inferiors show much humanity and some familiarity.' And 'Open not thy gate to flatterers, nor thine ears to backbiters.' Shakespeare made his character Polonius say in *Hamlet*:

> Be thou familiar, but by no means vulgar;
> The friends thou hast, and their adoption tried,
> Grapple them to thy soul with hoops of steel . . .
> . . . Beware
> Of entrance to a quarrel, but, being in,
> Bear't that th' opposed may beware of thee.
> Give every man thine ear, but few thy voice . . .

So Shakespeare's *Hamlet* was put to political use, as well as his *Richard II* and Marlowe's *Edward II*. Kit Marlowe and Shakespeare were broadly speaking in the same political faction, as the Walsinghams were connected with the Earl of Essex by Frances's marriage to him, and Shakespeare's patron the Earl of Southampton was one of Essex's most devoted adherents.

When Essex was building his importance at court he endeavoured to set up a personal spy service even better than that of his deceased father-in-law. To this end he employed two of

Burleigh's nephews, Anthony and Francis Bacon – a surprising choice, but they were loyal to Essex. The justification for the spy service was claimed to be the continuing hostility of Spain, and its support for a Catholic succession in England. In 1594, the year after Marlowe's death, Essex was to use Marlowe's play *The Jew of Malta* to stir up feeling against a Portuguese Jew he alleged was a spy. This man, Dr Lopez, was physician to Queen Elizabeth, and Essex claimed he intended to poison the Queen. Though the Queen called Essex 'a rash and temerarious youth' for arresting her doctor, and Robert Cecil had assured the Queen that the allegations could not be proved, Essex wrote to Anthony Bacon: 'The point of conspiracy was Her Majesty's death. The executioner should have been Dr Lopez; the manner poison. This I have so followed as I will make it appear as clear as the noon day.' And so he did. With Cecil he examined Dr Lopez and others in the Tower, and under torture enough circumstantial evidence was amassed to send Dr Lopez for trial and execution. London theatregoers saw in *The Jew of Malta* the Portuguese Jew getting his deserved punishment.

On 13 July 1592 Lord Strange's merged company put on a performance in Canterbury for the mayor, aldermen, council and local residents, for which the payment was thirty shillings – a good house. It is very likely that they staged Kit Marlowe's *The Jew of Malta*, and that some of the play's many Canterbury references date from this performance. The mention of the 'dark entry', for example, is apt from an old pupil of King's School as it was between the school and the cathedral through Prior Sellingegate; and the Jew sending poisoned broth into the nunnery through the 'dark entry' would help the audience to identify with the play. Another example was in Act v when

> Know Selim, that there is a monastery
> Which standeth as an out-house to the town

referred to the ruined St Augustine's Abbey, well known to Canterbury residents, where Kit Marlowe had played as a child.

Even 'out-house' was a word with Kent connotations.

Another telling example was the name of one of the ships in the argosy – 'The Flying Dragon' – as a ship of that name visited Dover harbour regularly in the 1560s, and Dover was only fifteen miles from Canterbury and easily visitable.

Some of the actors for this performance may have boarded with Kit's mother, as John Marlowe's establishment was close to where the performance took place. Kit was definitely in Canterbury in September, and probably came earlier to see the local performance of his play, remaining in Canterbury because of the plague which was virulent in London but had not yet reached Canterbury.

Kit quarrelled with a part-time musician at the cathedral, William Corkine, and a duel took place in which neither party was injured. However, they were taken to court where a reconciliation occurred. William Corkine's son, the lutenist of the same name, set Kit's lyric 'Come Live With Me and Be My Love' to music so the reconciliation became active cooperation.

Coincidentally, one of the most vocal Puritan opponents of the theatre had been born in the same Canterbury parish as Marlowe – Stephen Gosson, the writer, and son of Cornelius Gosson the joiner and his wife the grocer's daughter. Gosson attacked not only what took place on the stage, but the behaviour of the audience. He also criticized Roman audiences, but his most bitter words were for the London theatres.

... In our assemblies at plays in London, you shall see such heaving and shoving, such itching and shouldering, to sit by women .. Not that any filthiness in deed is committed within the compass of that ground, as was done in Rome, but that every wanton and his paramour ... every knave and his quean, are there first acquainted and cheapen the merchandise in that place, which they pay for elsewhere as they can agree.

Gosson attacked poets, players and 'such like caterpillars of a commonwealth', but if a play had a good moral it was excused.

Such a play was *The Jew*, which was one of the sources of Kit Marlowe's play. *The Jew*, said Gosson, exposed the 'greediness of worldly choosers'.

Something most distressing for Kit Marlowe happened in September 1592 – his friend Thomas Watson died. Life for Tom Watson had not been the same joyous affair since the Bradley affray and his consequent imprisonment, though he had written a memorial poem to Sir Francis Walsingham and published a book of madrigals since his release.

He was buried on 26 September in the churchyard of St Bartholomew-the-Less. His praises were sung in verse by fellow poets Spenser, Peele, Nashe, Lodge, Daniel, Clarke, the argumentative Harvey, and surprisingly and apparently unashamedly by Fraunce, who had earlier translated Watson's 'Amyntas' from Latin and passed it as his own poem. Kit Marlowe was still in Canterbury at the time of Watson's death, and his return would have been sad indeed when he heard the news of his friend's burial.

Kit Marlowe made his own memorial to Watson. He took Watson's new Latin poem 'Amyntae Gaudia' to the publishers, and dedicated it to the same person as Fraunce had chosen for his version of Watson's 'Amyntas' – the much sought-after patron Lady Sidney, Countess of Pembroke. It was a very moving dedication in which he referred to 'this posthumous Amyntas', which he urged Lady Sidney to treat as 'thine adoptive son: the rather that his dying father had most humbly bequeathed to thee his keeping'.

As Kit Marlowe's association with the Earl of Pembroke's players dates from this time, when they were staging *Edward II* and such contributions as he had made to other histories, his dedication of Watson's poem to Lady Sidney, though it was in payment of Watson's old debt, made a second interesting connection with the Pembroke household. Kit Marlowe probably had little to do with the son of the household, William Herbert, but William Herbert was to be the likely receiver of the dedication of Shakespeare's *Sonnets*, although in them Shakespeare actually referred to the Earl of Southampton. By the time the *Sonnets* had been printed by Thomas Thorpe, Southampton had been all but eclipsed following his part in the Essex revolt; but as Kit Marlowe was not only the rival poet of the *Sonnets** but was in Shakespeare's mind till his last solo play (*The Tempest*), the son of the patron of their joint playwright ventures was a likely dedicatee of these poems.

If the three-way swordfight in Shakespeare's *Romeo and Juliet* referred to Watson, Marlowe and Bradley, Shakespeare's portrait of Mercutio was his memorial to Watson, as the publication of 'Amyntae Gaudia' was Marlowe's gesture for his old friend.

Interesting speculation about what could have happened when Kit was in Canterbury in July–September 1592 centres round further researches of the indefatigable Dr William Urry. In the early 1600s, he discovered, a 'Joan Marlowe, widow' resided with Anne Cranford, Kit's sister who ran a somewhat seedy inn in Canterbury. Could this Joan Marlowe be Kit's widow? Was this why he was so touchy with William Corkine? Kit Marlowe's time in Canterbury in autumn 1592 may have been put to profitable use, in a way which made 'Come Live With Me and Be My Love' very relevant.

* See Chapter 15

14 · Doctor Faustus

Kit Marlowe's return from Canterbury was sad indeed. Tom Watson was dead. Robert Greene, not a friend but a long-time associate, was dead. There was plague.

But life continued. Marlowe's most mature play, *Edward II*, had been acted, and a new playwright, William Shakespeare, was becoming prominent. He and Marlowe were involved with the same company at this time, Pembroke's Men; and their poetry patrons, Thomas Walsingham in Kit Marlowe's case and the Earl of Southampton in Shakespeare's, were within the circle of the Earl of Essex.

Kit Marlowe was entering the final and most dramatic phase of his playwright's life.

Thomas Walsingham was also affected by the death of Tom Watson. Perhaps this was why, as well as because of the plague, Kit went to stay with his friend and patron at Scadbury in Chislehurst.

The plague was to reach its height in 1592–4, and was itself conducive to the dramatic death atmosphere of Kit's play *Doctor Faustus*, which he was now to finish. In such times death was sudden and usually inescapable, the cry echoing through deserted streets, 'Bring out your dead', underlining its finality. Bereavement and fatal disease were made worse by expectation – as Faustus expected his end.

Lord Pembroke's acting company was doubly affected by the plague; on tour in the country the troupe went bankrupt. They were forced to pawn their costumes because they could not 'save their charges with travel on the road', as Henslowe wrote to his son-in-law Edward Alleyn.

E

When Alleyn was on tour he wrote to his wife Joan ('My good sweet mouse') with advice on how death by plague might be avoided. 'Keep your house fair and clean . . . and every evening throw water before your door, and in your backside, and have in your windows good store of rue and herb of grace, and with all the grace of God, which must be obtained by prayers; and so doing, no doubt but the Lord will mercifully defend you . . .'

Kit's friend Thomas Nashe wrote a haunting poem about the plague, with the repeated line 'I am sick I must die', emphasizing its finality.

> Adieu, farewell earth's bliss,
> This world uncertain is;
> Fond are life's lustful joys,
> Death proves them all but toys,
> None from his darts can fly.
> I am sick, I must die.
> >> Lord have mercy on us!
>
> Rich men, trust not in wealth,
> Gold cannot buy you health;
> Physic himself must fade,
> All things to end are made.
> The plague full swift goes by;
> I am sick, I must die.
> >> Lord have mercy on us!
>
> Beauty is but a flower
> Which wrinkles will devour:
> Brightness falls from the air,
> Queens have died young and fair,
> Dust hath closed Helen's eye.
> I am sick, I must die.
> >> Lord have mercy on us!
>
> Strength stoops unto the grave,
> Worms feed on Hector brave,

Swords may not fight with fate.
Earth still holds ope her gate;
Come! come! the bells do cry.
I am sick, I must die.
          Lord have mercy on us!

Wit with his wantonness
Tasteth death's bitterness;
Hell's executioner
Hath no ears for to hear
What vain art can reply.
I am sick, I must die.
          Lord have mercy on us!

Haste, therefore, each degree,
To welcome destiny.
Heaven is our heritage,
Earth but a player's stage;
Mount we unto the sky.
I am sick, I must die.
          Lord have mercy on us!

Inescapability was much stressed at this time. In Act 1 of *Faustus*, Kit Marlowe had written:

What doctrine call you this? Che sera sera:
What will be, shall be! Divinity, adieu!

and this Italian proverb, without Marlowe's translation but with 'divinity, adieu', was quoted, ascribed to Faustus, among margin notes in Thomas Nashe's handwriting in a book by John Leland. The book was published in 1589 but it is not known when Nashe made the notes. Nashe's interest in Faustus points to his involvement with Marlowe at this time, particularly as Nashe was another of those warned by Greene's deathbed repentances, which made a deep impression on Marlowe when he was completing *Doctor Faustus*.

Kit's decision to finish *Doctor Faustus* was encouraged by a translation of the *Historia von D. Johan Fausten* (published in Frankfurt by an anonymous Lutheran in 1587), appearing in England in 1592. Its title page read: 'THE HISTORIE of the damnable life, and deserved death of Doctor John Faustus, Newly imprinted, and in convenient places imperfect matter amended: according to the true Copie printed at Frankfort, and translated into English by P. F. Gent. Seene and allowed. Imprinted by Thomas Orwin and to be solde by Edward White, dwelling at the little North doore of Paules, at the signe of the Gun. 1592.'

The translator 'P. F.' has not been identified and 'newly imprinted' suggests an earlier edition. This did not refer to 'A ballad of the life and deathe of Doctor FFAUSTUS the great Cunngerer', which was entered in the Stationers' Register on 28 February 1589 (though it would be interesting to learn about this lost work), but is explained by a court battle between Abell Jeffes and Tho. Orwin about the copyright of the German translation. As Tho. Orwin's edition was to be sold by Edward White, two of the same protagonists were involved as in a disagreement over the printing of Thomas Kyd's *The Spanish Tragedy*. Orwin claimed that 'one Richard Oliff' had entered the book in the Stationers' Register; but the court ruled that if the book had not been entered 'before Abell Jffs clamed the same wch was about May last', then Jeffes held the copyright. This was so, and the earlier edition from which the 'imperfect matter' was amended was that of Jeffes.

Court cases like this were frequent as Elizabethans were given to litigation – and to street fighting. When Kit Marlowe is thought lawless (because of his three court appearances), the record of some other Elizabethans should be remembered. Ben Jonson, for example, killed a man (the victim being confused with 'Mr Marlow' by John Aubrey) and among other brushes with the law was imprisoned with Nashe for writing 'seditious material'. Kit Marlowe barely drew blood; he was rescued by Watson in the Hog Lane fight, and was reconciled with Corkine in Canterbury after no injury had been done. By Elizabethan standards he was fairly gentle.

Much of Kit Marlowe's *Doctor Faustus* was based on P. F.'s translation. While Kit could have read the original German book, and no doubt saw 'A Ballad of the life and deathe of Doctor FFAUSTUS the great Cunngerer', there are many parallels between his play and the translated *Damnable Life*. So although Kit rewrote parts to round the play's structure, and though historical references, for example the 'fiery keel', point to work done in Armada time, the play relies mainly on the *Damnable Life*. Comparison of the prologues of Marlowe's 'The Tragical History of the Life and Death of Doctor Faustus' and the translated 'Historie of the Damnable Life, and Deserved Death of Doctor John Faustus' by P. F. demonstrates the way Kit Marlowe absorbed this material.

> Not marching in the fields of Trasimene
> Where Mars did mate the warlike Carthagens,
> Nor sporting in the dalliance of love
> In courts of kings where state is overturn'd,
> Nor in the pomp of proud audacious deeds
> Intends our muse to vaunt his heavenly verse:
> Only this, gentles – we must now perform
> The form of Faustus' fortunes, good or bad:
> And now to patient judgements we appeal,
> And speak for Faustus in his infancy.
> Now is he born, of parents base of stock,
> In Germany, within a town call'd Rhode;
> At riper years to Wittenberg he went,
> Whereas his kinsmen chiefly brought him up.
> So much he profits in divinity,
> The fruitful plot of scholarism grac'd,
> That shortly he was grac'd with doctor's name,
> Excelling all, and sweetly can dispute
> In th' heavenly matters of theology;

Till, swollen with cunning of a self-conceit,
His waxen wings did mount above his reach,
And, melting, heavens conspir'd his overthrow;
For, falling to a devilish exercise,
And gutted now with learning's golden gifts,
He surfeits upon cursed necromancy;
Nothing so sweet as magic is to him,
Which he prefers before his chiefest bliss:
And this the man that in his study sits.

Faustus, Prologue, 11–27.

D.L., i. *Iohn Faustus*, borne in the town of *Rhode*, lying in the Prouince of *Weimer* in *Germ[anie,]* his father a poore Husbandman, and not [able] wel to bring him vp: but hauing an Uncle at *Wittenberg*, a rich man, & without issue, took this *I. Faustus* from his father, & made him his heire, in so much that his father was no more troubled with him, for he remained with his Uncle at *Wittenberg*, where he was kept at yᵉ Uniuersitie in the same citie to study diuinity. But *Faustus* being of a naughty minde & otherwise addicted, applied not his studies, but tooke himselfe to other exercises ... he gaue himself secretly to study Necromancy and Coniuration, in so much that few or none could perceiue his profession.

But to the purpose: *Faustus* continued at study in the Uniuersity, & was by the Rectors and sixteene Masters afterwards examined howe he had profited in his studies; and being found by them, that none for his time were able to argue with him in Diuinity, or for the excellency of his wisedome to compare with him, with one consent they made him Doctor of Diuinitie.

D.L., ii. You haue heard before, that all *Faustus* minde was set to study the artes of Necromancie and Coniuration, the which exercise hee followed day and night: and taking to him the wings of an Eagle, thought to flie ouer the whole world, and to know the secrets of heauen and earth; for his Speculation was so wonderfull, being expert in vsing his *Vocabula*, Figures, Characters, Coniurations, and other Ceremoniall actions.

The first six lines of Marlowe's Prologue are in the vein of his Prologue to *Tamburlaine*, except for the reference to

Edward II ('the dalliance of love In courts of kings'), which could have been added later, and Faustus's humble birth is noted before it is stated that he was born in Rhodes. Marlowe does not say directly that Faustus's relative who paid for his education was his uncle, but calls him his kinsman who 'brought him up'; as Marlowe also had an uncle who helped with his education (Thomas Arthur) but who did not bring him up, he is not stressing the likeness between his own background and that of Faustus. Marlowe adapted 'the wings of the eagle' in the third paragraph of the *Damnable Life* to the Icarus story of melting wings (which was also applied by Talbot to his son in *Henry VI*, Part One).

Faustus is related to *Tamburlaine* because it is another grand theme. Tamburlaine is 'the scourge of God' and Faustus a man in revolt against God. Both are eventually punished.

In its way, *Faustus* is Kit Marlowe's complement to *Tamburlaine*. Tamburlaine conquered the known world and then death conquered him. Faustus conquered the supernatural world by selling his soul to Mephistophilis, but was a complete loser because he could not regain his soul.

One difference between Marlowe's play and the *Damnable Life* is the presence in the former of angels, who reason with Faustus. The German Faust book was a dour story, as Lutheranism usually was, and unembellished. As Kit's *Tamburlaine* had been full of the heavens, the stars and the angels ('now walk the angels on the walls of heaven') this sparkle continued into *Faustus*. Though a condemned sinner, Marlowe's Faustus saw glories and wonders during his lost years.

The parade of the Seven Deadly Sins in Marlowe's *Doctor Faustus* is not taken from the *Damnable Life*. This has a medieval atmosphere as well as being reminiscent of Greene's last warning. The sins were often represented pictorially, and are aptly placed in this part of the development of the Faustus story. As with his adaptation of Holinshed's chronicle for *Edward II*, Kit Marlowe was becoming adept at marshalling material.

When Kit Marlowe is anti-clerical it is usually the Catholics he attacks. In *Edward II* the bishops were regarded as people worthy of respect and Gaveston's behaviour to them as wrong. The Pope receives no such respect from Doctor Faustus. However, as the German Faust book had been compiled by an anti-papist Lutheran, Marlowe is less brutal to the Pope in his play than the Lutheran had been. Marlowe's Faustus makes some joke about the Pope's crossing himself ('Must every bit be spiced with a cross') and then 'hits him a box of the ear'. The Lutheran's Faustus 'smote' the Pope 'on the face'. In both, Faustus is cursed with bell, book and candle.

Occasionally Kit Marlowe's classicism breaks through. Horns are made to grow on Benvolio's head in both versions, but Kit Marlowe likens him to 'bold Actaeon' Shakespeare later borrowed this incident in *The Merry Wives of Windsor*, and acknowledged Kit Marlowe by misquoting his lyric 'Come Live With Me and Be My Love'.

Helen of Troy is in both versions, but while Kit Marlowe wrote most beautiful verse about her, the *Damnable Life* was initially more prosaic and later insulting. The *Damnable Life* says 'fayre Helena of Greece ... was more than commonly fayre, because when she was stolne away from her husband, there was for her recovery so great bloodshed ...' and '... he [Faustus] called his Spirit Mephistophiles, commanding him to bring him the faire Helena, which he also did. Whereupon he fel in love with her, & made her his common Concubine & bedfellow, for she was so beautiful and delightful a peece, that he could not be one houre from her ...' Kit Marlowe wrote:

> Was this the face that launch'd a thousand ships
> And burnt the topless towers of Illium? ...
> I will be in Paris, and for love of thee
> Instead of Troy shall Wittenberg be sack'd ...
> Oh, thou art fairer than the evening's air
> Clad in the beauty of a thousand stars ...

When Faustus approaches the time of retribution Kit Marlowe
wrote some of the greatest dramatic poetry in the English language.
The inevitable is brought terrifyingly close by the clock striking
eleven.

Ah, Faustus,
Now hast thou but one bare hour to live,
And then thou must be damn'd perpetually.
Stand still, you ever-moving spheres of heaven,
That time may cease, and midnight never come . . .
The stars move still, time runs, the clock will strike . . .
O, I'll leap up to my God! Who pulls me down?
See, see where Christ's blood streams in the firmament!
One drop would save my soul, half a drop . . .
Where is it now? 'Tis gone: and see where God
Stretcheth out his arm and bends his ireful brows.
Mountains and hills, come, come, and fall on me,
And hide me from the heavy wrath of God! . . .
No, no!
Then will I headlong run into the earth.
Earth, gape! O, no, it will not harbour me.
You stars that reign'd at my nativity,
Whose influence hath allotted death and hell,
Now draw up Faustus like a foggy mist
Into the entrails of yon labouring cloud . . .

O, it strikes, it strikes! Now, body, turn to air,
Or Lucifer will bear thee quick to hell!
      (Thunder and lightning)
O soul, be chang'd into little water drops,
And fall into the ocean, ne'er be found.
      (Enter devils.)
My God, my God! Look not so fierce on me!
Adders and serpents, let me breathe awhile!
Ugly hell, gape not! Come not, Lucifer;

I'll burn my books! – Ah, Mephistophilis!
(Exeunt with him.)

Significantly this complements *Tamburlaine*. 'Smile, stars that reign'd at my nativity' becomes 'You stars that reign'd at my nativity'. 'And set black streamers in the firmament' becomes 'See, see where Christ's blood streams in firmament'. 'Wrapt in the bowels of a freezing cloud' becomes 'Now draw up Faustus like a foggy mist/Into the entrails of yon labouring cloud'.

Faustus's last-breath offer to burn his books is like Shakespeare's Prospero breaking his staff in *The Tempest*, though Prospero succeeded where Faustus failed. *Doctor Faustus* has a deeper theme than *The Tempest*, but it is interesting to compare Shakespeare's magician with Faustus. Some think that Prospero was more like Dr John Dee than Faustus, but this is to judge Dee with hindsight. The reactions of Elizabethans to him were more those of the public to Faustus who 'deserved punishment', and Dee had his library of rare books at Mortlake burned by frightened crowds. Marlowe may be referring to this.

The Tempest was the most Rosicrucian of Shakespeare's works, and was one of the plays performed in May 1613 for King James's daughter and her husband the Prince Palatine Elector, who were involved with the Rosicrucian movement. *The Tempest* in a gentler way complements Marlowe's *Faustus*, as, written eighteen years later, it could view the rumbustious 1590s with detachment. Though incorporating some of the attributes of the masque, which Marlowe's plays never did, the spirits of these sequences are related to the spirits of *Faustus*, but are classical while Marlowe's were Christian. Judged by the religion of the time, Marlowe's *Faustus* was not atheistic, and Kit Marlowe is in the same danger as Dr John Dee of being misjudged by hindsight. Though Marlowe was in many ways a Renaissance man, Shakespeare's *The Tempest* is more Renaissance, and Marlowe's *Faustus* is more medieval. Marlowe's *Faustus* is also more medieval than the Lutheran *Damnable Life*.

Brought up in a cathedral city, and educated at King's School, attached to the cathedral, and at tradition-bound Cambridge, Kit Marlowe knew more of the medieval heritage than did Shakespeare or Jonson, and so did his friend Thomas Nashe, who had Marlowe so much in mind at this time. It is therefore not surprising that Shakespeare's play is the less Christian of the two. *The Tempest* is an agreeable fable and surprisingly echoes not only *Faustus* but *Tamburlaine*. For example:

> Over my zenith hang a blazing star (*Tambulaine*,
> Part Two, Act III)

becomes in *The Tempest*

> I find my zenith doth depend upon
> A most auspicious star . . .
> (*The Tempest*, Act I)

Ben Jonson's Alchemist is a different character, though descended from the Dr John Dee image. Worldly-wise Jonson knew about frauds, fakes and human gullibility. Marlowe and Shakespeare treated Faustus and Prospero with respect, even affection, and gave them, even Faustus, a kind of integrity. Ben Jonson's world is one of greedy people who deserved to be laughed at.

It was Jonson's image that persisted, through a whole string of funny plays about phoney alchemists, though none with the authority of Jonson's original. Perhaps there was no one of sufficient ability to emulate Marlowe and Shakespeare. Hindsight has been right to redress the balance in Dr John Dee's favour; but it has wrongly given him twentieth-century understanding.

Doctor Faustus, more than Kit Marlowe's other plays, demonstrates the promise yet to come. What would he have written in 1611, when Shakespeare was composing *The Tempest*?

As it was, his personal tragedy was drawing inexorably closer.

15 · The Rival Poets

Kit Marlowe's *Hero and Leander* was unfinished at his death, but this does not mean it was his last work. He may well have written the part he did complete in Canterbury, while he was waiting for his court appearance over the Corkine affair in the autumn of 1592, as the poem does not exude the plague and death atmosphere of *Doctor Faustus*. The plague did affect Canterbury badly, but reached its height in 1593; plague in London always reached Canterbury, but took a while to travel up the Dover road. It seems likely that it was work on *Doctor Faustus*, rather than *Hero and Leander*, which occupied Kit Marlowe when he went to stay with Thomas Walsingham at Scadbury, on his return from Canterbury. Faustus said in Scene i:

> Are not thy bills hung up as monuments,
> Whereby whole cities have escap'd the plague
> And thousand desperate maladies been cur'd?

However, Kit Marlowe must have shown *Hero and Leander* to his circle of acquaintances because it inspired the new playwright, William Shakespeare, to his first major work of verse, *Venus and Adonis*, which was registered in April 1593 and printed by his friend Richard Field. Marlowe's poem was not published until 1598, with Chapman's completion.

Though the poems are linked, Marlowe's unfinished one is the more accomplished. It is the work of a practised poet, while Shakespeare's is lively but uneven. There is a great difference between the heroines. Marlowe's Hero is gentle, ladylike, if occasionally spirited. Shakespeare's Venus is an overpowering country lady who makes the most of the running. Critics see Shakespeare's patron the Earl of Southampton in gentle, pursued Adonis, but it is also not hard to see Shakespeare's wife Anne Hathaway in Venus; and though he may be advising Southampton about marriage in the latter part of the poem, the earlier part reads like an apologia for what happened to Shakespeare himself – marrying an older woman because she was pregnant.

Kit Marlowe's gentlemanly treatment of Hero could have been influenced by his mother, if he stayed with his parents while he waited for his court appearance in Canterbury. Like many mothers she may have decided it was time her son 'settled down', and if Joan Marlowe were Kit's widow she may originally have been a girl chosen by his mother. He certainly showed awareness of female apparel in his description of Hero and his attitude to her was loverlike rather than brotherly.

> At Sestos Hero dwelt; Hero the fair,
> Whom young Apollo courted for her hair,
> And offered as a dower his burning throne,
> Where she should sit for men to gaze upon.
> The outside of her garments were of lawn,
> The lining purple silk, with gilt stars drawn;
> Her wide sleeves green, and bordered with a grove,
> Where Venus in her naked glory strove
> To please the careless and disdainful eyes
> Of proud Adonis that before her lies.
> Her kirtle blue, whereon was many a stain,
> Made with the blood of wretched lovers slain.
> Upon her head she ware a myrtle wreath,
> From whence her veil reached to the ground beneath.

Kit Marlowe's Hero was attracted to Leander but needed constant wooing. Leander was inexperienced 'and raw', and learned about love-making in the course of the wooing – which may be what happened to Kit Marlowe himself.

Albeit Leander, rude in love, and raw,
Long dallying with Hero, nothing saw
That might delight him more, yet he suspected
Some amorous rites or other were neglected.
Therefore unto his body hers he clung;
She, fearing on the rushes to be flung,
Strived with redoubled strength; the more she strived,
The more a gentle pleasing heat revived,
Which taught him all that elder lovers know.
And now the same 'gan so to scorch and glow,
As in plain terms (yet cunningly) he craved it;
Love always makes those eloquent that have it.

Shakespeare's lovers parted differently, with Adonis showing little sympathy for Venus:

> With this, he breaketh from the sweet embrace
> Of those fair arms which bound him to her breast,
> And homeward through the dark laund runs apace;
> Leaves Love upon her back, deeply distress'd.

Both poems are erotic, but Marlowe's is the more polished and loverlike. Shakespeare seemed relieved when he could get back to nature, and, for example, spent several verses describing a horse.

Both poems did have some tongue-in-cheek lines; there were many in-jokes between the literary fraternity at the time, for example Raleigh's 'reply' to Marlowe's 'Come Live With Me and Be My Love', and Donne's parody of it, about fishes. Marlowe's elaborate description of Leander's body was in this vein and has been misinterpreted by some critics who see homosexuality. There is certainly a sense of humour in his most outrageous lines.

> His body was straight as Circe's wand;
> Jove might have sipped out nectar from his hand.
> Even as delicious meat is to the taste,
> So was his neck in touching, and surpassed

The white of Pelops' shoulder. I could tell ye
How smooth his breast was, and how white his belly,
And whose immortal fingers did imprint
That heavenly path with many a curious dint
That runs along his back, but my rude pen
Can hardly blazon forth the loves of men,
Much less of powerful gods: let it suffice
That my slack muse sings of Leander's eyes,
Those orient cheeks and lips . . .

There is an emphasis on never having known love, and on find-
ing love, in the next lines.

The men of wealthy Sestos, every year,
For his sake whom their goddess held so dear,
Rose-cheeked Adonis, kept a solemn feast.
Thither resorted many a wand'ring guest
To meet their loves; such as had none at all
Came lovers home from this great festival.

Shakespeare's nature descriptions were the more realistic, but
Marlowe wrote of love-making with greater detail and more
delicacy.

Herewith affrighted Hero shrunk away,
And in her lukewarm place Leander lay,
Whose lively heat, like fire from heaven fet,
Would animate gross clay, and higher set
The drooping thoughts of base declining souls
Than dreary Mars carousing nectar bowls.
His hands he cast upon her like a snare . . .
Yet there with Sisyphus he toiled in vain,
Till gentle parley did the truce obtain.
Wherein Leander on her quivering breast
Breathless spoke something, and sighed out the rest;
Which so prevailed . . .

Kit Marlowe is never more clearly seen than when something he wrote is compared with a related work by someone else. Comparison of *Doctor Faustus* with the translated *Damnable Life*, on which most of it was based, shows Kit Marlowe softening the blows, thus belying the accusation that he was always a stirrer. Comparison of *Hero and Leander* with *Venus and Adonis* reveals Kit Marlowe as more polished, and more diffident, than Shakespeare was at that time. Chapman's completion of Marlowe's *Hero and Leander*, competent, benevolent and classically correct, points up the spiritedness and slight ingenuousness of Marlowe's part.

Both *Venus and Adonis* and *Hero and Leander* have sad endings, which Marlowe avoided by leaving his part unfinished. If he were in the flush of first love he would not want to contemplate his own death, as occurred to unfortunate Leander and Adonis. It is ironic that Marlowe himself was to die, while Shakespeare and Chapman continued to mellow middle age. The suggestion that the dedication of Marlowe's verses to Thomas Walsingham (and Chapman's completion to Audrey Walsingmam when the parts were published together) was a wedding gift to the Walsinghams seems strange when the poetic lovers met such a fate; though if it were a memorial to Marlowe this makes more sense. Shakespeare's poem, published several years earlier, was printed by his friend Richard Field while Marlowe's must have circulated in manuscript.

Musaeus had been the basis of the story of *Hero and Leander*, and Ovid for *Venus and Adonis*, though Marlowe's *Hero and Leander* had Ovidean overtones. In fact, it would seem that Shakespeare feared Marlowe's description of Leander, which was thought to apply to Shakespeare's patron the Earl of Southampton, dimmed his own poetic enterprise. When Marlowe's poem was published his friends made certain this misunderstanding was cleared up by dedicating it to his true patron Thomas Walsingham.

Shakespeare said:

> But when your countenance filled up his line,
> Then lacked I matter; that enfeebled mine.

and these lines come from Shakespeare's 'rival poet' sonnet which has been the source of much speculation. The other poet can definitely be established as Kit Marlowe when Shakespeare's sonnet is compared with Thomas Thorpe's letter of dedication (to Edward Blout) of Marlowe's translation of the First Book of Lucan, in 1600. Shakespeare's sonnet contains a paraphrase of Thorpe's words about 'that pure elementall wit, Chr. Marlow'. Thorpe said that Marlowe's 'ghoast or Genius is to be seene walke the Churchyard in (at the least) three or foure sheets. Me thinks you should presently looke wilde now, and grow humourously frantique upon the tast of it . . . This spirit was sometimes a familiar of your own.'

Shakespeare said:

> Was it his spirit, by spirits taught to write
> Above a mortal pitch, that struck me dead?
> No, neither he, nor his compeers by night
> Giving him aid, my verse astonished.
> He nor that *affable familiar ghost*
> Which nightly gulls him with intelligence,
> As victors of my silence cannot boast;
> I was not sick of any fear from thence . . .

Shakespeare was not afraid, even humorously, of the 'familiar ghost', familiar being a pun on magician's familiars, as in Faustus and as used by Thorpe, but he knew Marlowe's verse was superior to his own.

This shows that Sonnet 86 was *about* the 1593 period, but quill was probably not put to paper until around 1600 when Thorpe wrote his dedication of Marlowe's Lucan to Blout. Shakespeare may have seen Thorpe's manuscript, as Thorpe was also a friend of Shakespeare and was the man who printed the

F

Sonnets in 1609, but Shakespeare could not have seen the Marlowe/Lucan introduction in 1593.

The one new word Shakespeare added to his paraphrase of Thorpe's 'Marlowe' passage was 'affable' – Shakespeare had not found Marlowe personally difficult. He may have feared Marlowe's ability to overshadow his work, but Kit had not been unkind.

Nevertheless, the misunderstanding that by describing Southampton as Leander Marlowe looked to Southampton as a patron was reflected in several sonnets. In Sonnet 79:

> Yet what of thee thy Poet doth invent,
> He robs thee of, and payes it thee againe,
> He lends thee vertue, and he stole that word
> From thy behaviour, beautie doth he give
> And found it in thy cheeke . . .

Marlowe had written:

> For his sake whom their goddess held so dear,
> Rose-cheeked Adonis . . .

If it were fear of Kit Marlowe stealing his poetry patron that drove Shakespeare to his first long poetic enterprise, inspiring him to publish *Venus and Adonis* instantly and dedicate it to Southampton, then rivalry between Marlowe and Shakespeare was productive from Shakespeare's point of view. And Shakespeare realized this. He began Sonnet 86:

> Was it the proud full sail of his great verse,
> Bound for the prize of (all too precious you),
> That did my ripe thoughts in my braine inhearse,
> Making their tombe the wombe wherein they grew?

The last poem in this sequence, Sonnet 87, refers to Marlowe's disappearance, and the unrivalled position in which Shakespeare now found himself. Shakespeare was grateful, which sheds a little light on what happened in 1593.

Farewell! Thou art too deare for my possessing,
And like enough thou knowst thy estimate,
The charter of thy worth gives thee releasing:
My bonds in thee are all determinate . . .

The cause of this fair gift in me is wanting . . .

They selfe thou gav'st, thy own worth not then knowing . . .

Shakespeare had sixteen years to feel guilty about blaming and misjudging Kit Marlowe by thinking he sought Southampton as a patron. This may be why the leading character of Shakespeare's last complete play, Prospero, was a version of the main character of Marlowe's last play, Faustus. Prospero then broke his staff, and the 'revels were over'.

16 · Scadbury

On 5 May 1593, between 11 pm and 12 midnight, rude verses were pinned on the wall of the Dutch churchyard in London. During the plague, when hardship was almost impossible to bear, discontent flared against foreign merchants like the Dutch, who were earning English money. The authorities, anxious to keep the peace, visited people who might be responsible for the verses. One of these was Thomas Kyd, the playwright, who once shared a room with Kit Marlowe; Kyd had recently been involved with writers who were working on a play (about Thomas More) highlighting Londoners' discontent against foreigners. One verse from it read:

> You strangers that inhabit in this land,
> Note this same writing, do it understand;
> Conceive it well for safeguard of your lives,
> Your goods, your children and your dearest wives.

Though the theatres were closed because of the plague, they had briefly opened the previous December, and would be able to stage a new play reflecting the public's mood immediately the disease subsided.

The authorities dealing with the Dutch churchyard affairs were instructed to search 'chambers, studies, chestes, or other like places for al manner of writings or papers that may geve you light for the discoverie of the libellers'. Among Kyd's effects they discovered a manuscript copy of a treatise on the beliefs of Arius – which they confiscated on grounds of heresy and atheism. Though this was in a 'noverint's hand', meaning that Kyd had copied it out himself, he claimed that it belonged to Marlowe. It had been 'shuffled with some of myne (unknown to me) by some occasion of o^r writinge in one chamber twoe years synce', as he claimed to Sir John Puckering later in a letter. Kyd was arrested, sent to Bridewell prison under the authority of the Star Chamber and probably tortured; heresy and atheism were serious charges.

The papers found in Kyd's room were labelled: 'vile hereticall Conceipts Denyinge the Deity of Jhesus Christ our Saviour fownd emongst the papers of Thos kydd prisoner'. In different writing was added: 'which he affirmeth that he had ffrom Marlowe'.

To do Kyd justice, he may have copied out the treatise for Marlowe; though if it had been unnoticed in Kyd's papers for two years then Marlowe could not have valued it enough to try to find it, or Kyd had hidden it for some reason. Kyd blamed Marlowe when the document was found, but had not previously taken steps to return it to Marlowe. Either Kyd was purposely keeping some of Marlowe's material, or Marlowe had no further use for the document, or both.

The last part of Kit Marlowe's life must not be approached with preconceived ideas. Because Greene had earlier accused Marlowe of atheism and a detractor accused him of it in 1593, it is sometimes assumed that atheism *was* Marlowe's view in 1593, though Kyd specifically said 'two years since', laying himself open to criticism that he had had two years to get rid of the document. Kyd is usually found to tell some, if not all, of the truth, and no doubt it *was* two years since Marlowe had been concerned with the heretical tract. The writing of *Hero and Leander* and *Doctor Faustus*, and the deaths of Greene and Watson had happened since then to modify his views.

Because Marlowe's life ended when he was young it is easy to forget that death does not mean a person has completed his development. Though it would be pure speculation to imagine what Kit Marlowe might have been at fifty, the way he was developing at twenty-nine is clear from a comparison of the *Damnable Life of Doctor John Faustus* with Marlowe's *Faustus*, showing him softening, not stirring, and of his *Hero and Leander* with Shakespeare's *Venus and Adonis*, showing him as both more polished and more diffident than country-bred Shakespeare. To pigeon-hole Marlowe as outspoken and 'atheist' does not give a true picture of the man in 1593, while it could have been true of him eighteen months before. John Donne, for example, is known as much for his later 'No Man is an Island' sermon as for his love poetry, and no one accepts a static picture of Donne at twenty-eight as the man who was preaching. Marlowe was changing at twenty-nine, even if he was only eighteen months away from his earlier excesses. It is Kit Marlowe's tragedy that when the Arian tract was found in Kyd's papers he was close enough to his outspoken period for this still to be in people's minds.

While Kyd was in Bridewell prison, Kit Marlowe was at Scadbury, Thomas Walsingham's home outside London, where they missed the mainstream of the plague. Not all playwrights and poets had such a helpful accommodating patron, and Kyd envied Marlowe his well-connected friend. The authorities knew where to find Marlowe when they went to apprehend him. Who told them? Kyd?

On 18 May a Henry Maunder received a warrant for the apprehension of Christopher Marlowe, according to a Privy Council entry. It read:

Warrant to Henry Maunder one of the Messengers of her Ma[es] Chamber to repaire to the house of Mr Tho: Walsingham in Kent, or to anie other place where he shall understand Christofer Marlow to be remayning, and by vertue hereof to apprehend and bring him to the Court in his Companie. And in case of need to require ayd.

Apparently it had been decided to confront Marlowe with being the owner of the tract. The fact that Marlowe was residing with Thomas Walsingham was in his favour as, though Sir Francis

Walsingham was dead, the family was still highly respected, and Frances, Thomas's cousin, was the wife of the popular Earl of Essex.

Marlowe must have satisfied the authorities that he was not a dangerous heretic as he was allowed to return to Scadbury as long as he reported to their lordships daily. The Privy Council entry for 20 May read:

This day Christofer Marley of London, gent, being sent for by warrant from their L(ordshi)ps, hath entered his apparance accordinglie for his Indemnity herein; and is commanded to give his daily attendance on their L(ordships), untill he shalbe lycensed to the Contrary.

He had to attend daily until he was licensed to the contrary; that is, he was not in danger of imminent imprisonment. There was no danger of his revealing secrets of Essex's espionage service under torture, and the Cecils could anyway have found this out by applying pressure on Anthony Bacon who was Lord Burleigh's nephew.

The fact that Kit Marlowe had done some secret-agent work in 1587 – the year before the Armada attacked England – does not mean that he was still seriously involved with this kind of government service in 1593. The main reason for the intense espionage network of Sir Francis Walsingham had disappeared with the defeat of the Armada, though there were scares of further Spanish attacks. Essex was building up his network, but this was aimed at making himself superior to the Cecils in Queen Elizabeth's eyes – which he demonstrated by the Lopez affair the next year, making use of Kit Marlowe's play *The Jew of Malta* in stirring up support for his accusations against this Portuguese Jew.

So there was little reason for the Walsingham household to be seriously worried about Marlowe's daily trips to the Privy Council; the heresy charge had not yet been proved, nor could be proved, as the tract was in a 'noverint's hand' and the accusation depended on Kyd's word that the document was Marlowe's – Kyd, who *was* a noverint, and was imprisoned while Marlowe merely made daily reports to the Privy Council.

However, the visits to the Privy Council would be time-consuming for Marlowe, and made him more vulnerable to an attack of the plague which he had left London to avoid. This was the greatest hazard in Kyd's accusation: Marlowe was forced to leave the clean air of Scadbury.

Originally it was known that Kit Marlowe had died in 1593, and that Gabriel Harvey, whose brother was the rector at Chislehurst, had said that he died of the 'grand disease'. Later his detractors – Richard Baines (from a seminary background and though a government informer seemingly with Catholic sympathies) and other assorted Puritans and Catholics over the next fifteen years – wrote of a shocking death. His friends and colleagues were upset by his death, but did not 'defend' him or even appear to take the accusations seriously. There are no refutations, only loving memories, and in the case of some, like Nashe and Shakespeare, guilt over having misunderstood Marlowe.

The inquest document Dr Hotson discovered should be examined thoroughly.

Kent/Inquisition Indented taken at Detford Strand in the aforesaid County of Kent within the verge on the first day of June in the year of the reign of Elizabeth by the grace of God of England France & Ireland Queen defender of the faith &c thirty fifth, in the presence of William Danby, Gentleman, Coroner of the household of our said lady the Queen, upon view of the body of Christopher Morley, there lying dead & slain, upon oath of Nicholas Draper, Gentleman, Wolstan Randall, gentleman, William Curry, Adrian Walker, John Barber, Robert Baldwyn, Giles ffeld, George Halfepenny, Henry Awger, James Batt, Henry Bendyn, Thomas Batt senior, John Baldwyn, Alexander Burrage, Edmund Goodcheepe, & Henry Dabyns . . .

[On 30 May] about the tenth hour before noon [the aforesaid gentlemen] met together in a room in the house of a certain Eleanor

Bull, widow; & there passed the time together & dined & after dinner were in quiet sort together there & walked in the garden belonging to the said house until the sixth hour after noon of the same day & then returned from the said garden to the room aforesaid & there together and in company supped; & after supper the said Ingram & Christopher Morley were in speech & uttered one to the other divers malicious words for the reason that they could not be at one nor agree about the payment of the sum of pence, that is, *le recknynge*, there; & the said Christopher Morley then lying upon a bed in the room where they supped, & moved with anger against the said Ingram ffrysar upon the words aforesaid spoken between them, and the said Ingram then & there sitting in the room aforesaid with his back towards the bed where the said Christopher Morley was then lying, sitting near the bed, that is, *nere the bed*, & with the front part of his body towards the table & the aforesaid Nicholas Skeres & Robert Poley sitting on either side of the said Ingram in such a manner that the same Ingram ffrysar in no wise could take flight: it so befell that the said Christopher Morley on a sudden & of his malice towards the said Ingram aforethought, then & there maliciously drew the dagger of the said Ingram which was at his back, and with the same dagger the said Christopher Morley then & there maliciously gave the aforesaid Ingram two wounds on his head of the length of two inches & of the depth of a quarter of an inch; whereupon the said Ingram, in fear of being slain, & sitting in the manner aforesaid between the said Nicholas Skeres & Robert Poley so that he could not in any wise get away, in his own defence & for the saving of his life, then & there struggled with the said Christopher Morley to get back from him his dagger aforesaid; in which affray the same Ingram could not get away from the said Christopher Morley; and so it befell in that affray that the said Ingram, in defence of his life, with the dagger aforesaid to the value of 12*d*. gave the said Christopher then & there a mortal wound over his right eye of the depth of two inches & of the width of one inch; of which mortal wound the aforesaid Christopher Morley then & there instantly died . . .

The jurors agreed that Frizer had 'killed and slew' Christopher Morley, and had not 'fled nor withdrew himself'.

The victim is called Christopher Morley, and while Kit Marlowe had been known as 'Morley' in the document which established his government service in 1587, ever since he was always 'Marley' (which he signed himself), some version of Marlowe (Marlow, Marlo, Marloe), or sometimes Marlin. 'Morley' was a common name in Elizabethan England. At Cambridge there had been another 'Christopher Morley' (at Trinity College) during Marlowe's time – a fact established by Dr Hotson himself – this Morley becoming a seminary priest. A Christopher Morley worked for Lady Mary Sidney as tutor. A Morley was named to Lord Burleigh as a bearer of confidential dispatches from agents and ambassadors in a letter from Utrecht on 2 October 1587; this was not Kit Marlowe, who was then completing *Tamburlaine*, Part Two. Another Morley wrote madrigals.

Who were the other three people involved in this affair?

Robert Poley was a spy of vast experience and long standing. He had played a vital part in the Babington Plot of 1586 and such a devious one that it was not always clear which side he was on. Eventually he was responsible for Mary's downfall by gaining Babington's confidence, Babington thinking he was on Mary's side; Poley then gave Babington's information to Sir Francis Walsingham. Poley 'attended Mr Thomas Walsingham for my secret recourse to Mr Secretary' at Sir Francis's house in Seething Lane; following this Ballard, another of the conspirators, was arrested at Poley's house. Poley's travels as a court messenger can be traced by the payments to him, and here a mystery is encountered. According to a warrant for Poley's payment he was supposedly not at Deptford at all on 30 May 1593, but at The Hague. The warrant read: '. . . the carryinge of letters in poste for Her Majesties speciall and secrete afaires of great importance from the Courte of Croydon.' He left for The Hague on 8 May, delivering the answers on 8 June (and receiving a payment of thirty shillings).

There were at least two Nicholas Skeres. One belonged to a

band of 'maisterles men & cut-purses, whose practice is to robbe Gentlemen's chambers and Artificers' shoppes in and about London', as mentioned by William Fleetwood, recorder of London, in a report to Lord Burleigh in July 1585. It is unlikely that this was the Skeres at Deptford. A 'Skyrres' was in Poley's company on 2 August 1586, when he was involved with the Babington affair. Then there was a Nicholas Skeres who was the second son of a merchant-tailor of that name, in the parish of All-Hallows-the-Less. Nicholas and his brother Jerome were Matthew Royden's securities in a bond to a goldsmith for the payment of £40 in February 1582. Kyd mentioned Royden as an associate of Marlowe eleven years later, but this is a tenuous connection between Kit Marlowe and the younger Skeres brother. There is a record of payment to a Nicholas Skeres for carrying important letters between the court and the Earl of Essex in 1589. This sounds like the Skeres of Deptford.

Ingram Frizer was employed by Thomas Walsingham as a business agent, and was the one who struck the fatal blow to Christopher Morley. He had been involved in 1591 with a Nicholas Skeres, presumably the one at Deptford, in a case of 'conny catching' in which a Drew Woodleffe from Aylesbury was tricked out of £200. Their behaviour was not unlike some of the clowns' actions in *Doctor Faustus*.

Was it Christopher Marlowe who met this unlikely trio at Eleanor Bull's house at Deptford? They gathered at the tenth hour before noon – i.e. 10 am. *This does not give Kit Marlowe time to have paid his daily visit to the Privy Council.* They were together until the sixth hour after noon, a total of eight hours. What did they discuss for all this time if it were not the one subject they had in common, espionage? Frizer, as servant to Thomas Walsingham, must have been involved in his master's activities, and why otherwise would Poley make a secret visit from the Low Countries – though this does establish why the meeting was at Deptford, a port Poley could reach easily, and not far from Scadbury where Frizer resided.

At this stage it seems Christopher Marlowe was not involved at all, and the fourth person was Morley, a spy from the Netherlands (perhaps the one named to Burleigh in 1587), who had made the trip across with Poley. Frizer and Skeres, now involved with the Earl of Essex, were secretly meeting two of the official spies. This Morley would not take kindly to being asked to pay the reckoning for two meals and refreshments for four by the 'conny-catching' Frizer and Skeres. A fight would ensue and the result be as described.

A body would have to be accounted for – an embarrassing body which should have been in the Low Countries.

Deptford was only a few miles from Chislehurst and Frizer would be known as Thomas Walsingham's servant; and it would also be known locally that the famous playwright Kit Marlowe was staying with Thomas Walsingham at Chislehurst. If Ingram Frizer, shaken, said the body of Morley was within the house, it would not be hard for the misapprehension to arise that this was Christopher Marlowe. Nor would wily Frizer take long in seeing the advantages of this misapprehension.

The inquest does not have to be 'explained away' or 'reinterpreted'. Because of the plague the body needed urgent burial, and Frizer and the other spies told the truth to the hastily assembled jurors next day. The body, called Christopher Morley, stabbed in the face so that it was unrecognizable, was seen by all sixteen. There is no comment about the profession of the deceased in the document. It was agreed that Ingram Frizer stabbed Christopher Morley in self-defence.

The burial entry was less accurate. The body was called 'Christopher Marlowe slain by *Francis* Frizer'.

Poley returned to The Hague, hoping the court would not discover that he had left there, as Frizer had shouldered the blame for the fatal stroke and his name alone, if incorrectly given, appeared in the burial register. Frizer had the fortune to be employed by a powerful master whose credit was high in a place so near Chislehurst. The spy Morley would be considered to have died abroad, and the body at Deptford was accounted for.

So there were no substituted sailors, no political murders – in fact, there was no need for Kit Marlowe to disappear at all. The need was to account for the murdered body already present, and Kit, unfortunately, most nearly fitted the bill. Doubtless someone rode hastily to Scadbury and told Thomas Walsingham and Kit the whole story.

Thomas Walsingham stood by Frizer and Skeres in the matter of the cony-catching; and there wasn't much he could do in this case as it was already a *fait accompli*. Marlowe would have to lie low at Chislehurst, at least let off from his daily attendances at the Privy Council. From Frizer's point of view, 'Marlowe' couldn't appear as the name of the victim till Kit had not appeared at the Privy Council – hence the burial register could be 'Marlowe' while the inquest had to be 'Morley' – in case there was some slip-up. Though Marlowe had earlier been called Morley once, and was still often called Marley, the *plays* usually bore the Marlowe spelling in some form, and this distinguished him from the spy Morley. As it was, Baines's 'informing' note was ambivalent about the actual day of Marlowe's disappearance.

Did Frizer have some hold on Thomas Walsingham so that his master always supported him? It could have been about lady friends, as Thomas may already have formed his 'attachment' with Audrey Shelton, who was a relative of Queen Elizabeth on her Boleyn side and a tactical match, and from Forman's diaries it is known that at least one lady was Thomas's 'mistress'. Frizer was later to manipulate shady business deals for Lady Audrey Walsingham herself.

If this is what happened then Kit Marlowe would have been furious about Frizer's actions. Baines heard of the entry in the burial register at Deptford, and changed his submission. The title was altered to 'A Note delivered on Whitson eve last of the most horrible blasphemes uttered by Cristofer Marley who within iii days after came to a soden and fearful end of his life'.

What did happen to Kit Marlowe, who had returned full of hope to meet one tragedy after another – the plague, Tom Watson's death, Kyd's betrayal, Frizer's chicanery, Thomas Walsingham's weakness?

Someone took Marlowe's *Edward II* to be published three weeks after the Deptford affray. It was a great pity this was not also done with *The Massacre at Paris* and *The Jew of Malta*.

Marlowe revised the conclusion of *Doctor Faustus*, which would now have meaning for himself. With enormous irony, after

> Fair nature's eye, rise, rise again and make
> Perpetual day; or let this hour be but
> A year, a month, a week, a natural day
> That Faustus may repent, and save his soul

he quoted from Ovid's *Amores*, I, xiii, 40

> O lente, lente currite, noctis equi!

– when the poet longs for everlasting night with his lover. If Marlowe met Joan only months before this, Frizer had done him a most cruel turn.

Did he at this time work on a draft of *Macbeth*? *Macbeth* is mistakenly thought to celebrate James ascending the throne, but it was also important as propaganda, supporting his right to succeed Elizabeth, with its prophecy of Banquo's descendants inheriting. Essex eventually aimed to be the successor himself, but Marlowe would not now favour the earl whose spies had used his name to cover the awful consequence of their meeting with Morley and Poley. Marlowe had, according to Kyd, shown interest in the court of Scotland and could well have been drawn to the Macbeth story, which was in the Holinshed chronicles where he had found *Edward II*.

The likeness of Lady Macbeth's remorse to Alice Arden's in *Arden of Faversham*, and its absence from the source material in

Holinshed's chronicles, has been noted. Sigmund Freud, the pioneering psychoanalyst, also remarks on this absence in *Some Character-types Met with in Psycho-analytical Work* (1916), and refers to Macbeth's own childlessness, which he compares with Queen Elizabeth's: 'The "virginal" Elizabeth, of whom it was rumoured that she had never been capable of child-bearing and who had once described herself as "a barren stock" in an anguished outcry at the news of James's birth, was obliged by this very childlessness of hers to make the Scottish king her successor.' In *Macbeth*, Act II, Macbeth said:

> Upon my head they placed a fruitless crown,
> And put a barren sceptre in my gripe,
> Thence to be wrenched with an unlineal hand,
> No son of mine succeeding. If it be so,
> For Banquo's issue have I filed my mind . . .

Kit Marlowe of course did not complete *Macbeth*, if he worked on a draft at this time. But it has a number of Marlowe 'references' as well as Lady Macbeth's remorse resembling that of Alice Arden, and it deals with being doomed to childlessness, as he was.

Edward Blout said, in the introduction to *Hero and Leander*, about Marlowe's death: 'When we have brought the breathless body to the earth; for albeit the eye there taketh his ever farewell of that beloved object, yet the impression of the man that hath been dear unto us, living an after life in our memory, there putteth us in mind of father obsequies due unto the deceased'. This does not sound like the burial of Morley at Deptford but has different settings, and the 'after life in our memory' is significant.

There was a tomb, old and unnamed, in the grounds of Scadbury. This could be where the body of Christopher Marlowe was buried by his friends when he died soon after Deptford, with Gabriel Harvey's brother officiating, Edward Blout helping to bring 'his breathless body to the earth', and Shakespeare having this sad occasion in mind when he set the scene for Ophelia's burial in *Hamlet*. If this were so, it leads to the awesome speculation that Marlowe took his own life in despair, because of the desolation of anonymity spreading out before him.

17 · Aftermath

The attacks on Kit Marlowe's reputation following the Deptford register entry that he had been 'slain by Francis Frizer' were two-fold: Richard Baines's note, and Kyd's letters to Sir John Puckering. Neither was circulated to the general public. Baines was an informer and Kyd was trying to clear his own name. Anonymity was Marlowe's fate in June 1593, not instant vilification; but these pieces of correspondence sowed the seed for sporadic vilification over the next hundred years, and have attained an importance beyond their merit.

The first revelation in Baines's allegations was the placing of Marlowe in Raleigh's circle, though he was credited with Hariot's work about Old Testament chronology. Baines claimed Marlowe said 'that the Indians and many Authors of antiquity have assuredly writen above 16 thousand years agone where as Adam is proved to have lived w'hin 6 thousand yeares', and praised Hariot 'that Moyses was but a Jugler, & that one Heriots being Sir W Raleighs man can do more than he'.

Two relevant facts emerge from this. The source of Baines's information is not given other than as Marlowe talking in Raleigh's circle, and Baines could not conceivably have been a member and have heard the remarks first-hand; and Hariot has turned out to be right, as Old Testament chronology is not scientifically accurate. So modern writers who claim that Marlowe was an atheist, and cite Baines, fly in the face of what they themselves believe. This had not been done with, say, Raleigh and Shakespeare, and Marlowe deserves better treatment. It is an example of how some writers want to paint Marlowe blacker than he was.

Baines made an allegation that foreshadowed Nietzsche.

Marlowe was supposed to have said 'that the beginning of Religion was only to keep men in awe'. This again sounds more like Hariot than the author of *Doctor Faustus*, who was genuinely in awe of divine retribution.

Contradictory remarks follow.

> That it was an easy matter for Moyses being brought vp in all the artes of the Egiptians to abuse the Jewes being a rude & grosse people.
> That Christ was a bastard and his mother dishonest.
> That he was the sonne of a Carpenter, and that if the Jewes among whome he was borne did Crucify him theie best knew him and whence he Came.

'The Jewes being a rude & grosse people' is an accusation which might be levelled against the author of *The Jew of Malta*. But the same Jews are imputed to have judgement: 'they best knew him and whence he Came'. These are examples of irreligious remarks which a Catholic of the Elizabethan period liked to describe as 'Protestant'. Protestants, to informers of Baines's Catholic sympathies, were irreligious; Elizabeth's court should return to the true religion, or ensure this by naming a Catholic successor.

Papist sympathies are then imputed to Marlowe.

> That if there be any god or any good religion, then it is in the papistes because the service of god is performed wth more Ceremonies, as Elevation of the mass, organs, singing men, Shaven Crownes & cta.
> that all protestantes are Hypocriticall asses.

In Baines's picture Marlowe is inconsistent, to say the least! There are other irreligious allegations, and then the two, again inconsistent, about homosexuality.

> That St John the Evangelist was bedfellow to C[hrist] and leaned alwaies in his bosome, that he vsed him as the sinners of *Sodoma*.
> That all they that loue not *Tobacco* & Boies were fooles.

Another alleged 'belief' contains praise of Catholic-type ceremonial, mixed with a reference to pipe-smoking.

That if Christ would haue instituted the sacrament wth more Ceremoniall Reverence it would haue bin had in more admiration, that it
would haue bin much better being administered in a *Tobacco* pipe.

Baines concludes:

These thinges, wth many other shall by good & honest witnes be
aproved to be his opinions and Comon Speeches, and that this Marlow
doth not only hould them himself, but almost into every Company
he Cometh he perswades men to *Atheism* willing them not to be
afeard of bugbeares and hobgoblins, vtterly scorning both god and
his ministers as J Richard Baines will Justify & approue both by mine
oth and the testimony of many honest men, and almost al men with
whome he hath Conversed any time will testify the same, and as I
think all men in Christianity ought to indevor that the mouth of so
dangerous a member may be stopped, he saith likewise that he hath
quoted a number of Contraieties oute of the Scripture wch he hath
giuen to some great men who in Convenient time shalbe named. When
these thinges shalbe Called in question the witnes shalbe produced.

Baines had begun preparing the allegations when he knew Marlowe was accused of atheism and was appearing before the Privy
Council. He received an unexpected gift about the evil ways of
Protestants (against which his efforts were aimed) when he heard
of the entry at Deptford. That Marlowe's friends did not respond
was probably because they did not know of Baines's allegations.
Others of Raleigh's circle were to be accused the next year of
atheism, and to be 'examined' at Cerne Abbas.

Kyd's first letter to Sir John Puckering has already been quoted,
as Kyd and Marlowe were 'writinge in one chamber twoe years
synce' and Kyd knew more about Marlowe than Baines. Kyd
explained that he came to meet Marlowe when working for the
same troupe of players.

The main reason for Kyd's first letter was to claim that he, Kyd,
was unjustly accused of atheism and that Marlowe owned the
offending paper. Even then he only said: 'to cleere my selfe of
being thought an Atheist, which *some* will sweare he was.' Not
everyone would accuse Marlowe of atheism.

Kyd went on to describe the wide-ranging discussions of Marlowe, 'Harriot, Warner, Royden, and some stationers of Paules churchyard'. Hariot, a scholar of considerable standing, thus appeared in both sets of accusations. In fact Kyd's second letter, unsigned, demonstrates probable collusion with Baines. Kyd's first two points are similar to two in Baines's list, but in the second Paul has become the juggler, not Moses. If Baines contrived a meeting with Kyd in prison, perhaps they could not hear each other clearly

The two points were:

1. He would report St John to be o^r savio^r Christes *Alexis* I cover it wth reverence and trembling that is that Christ did loue him wth an extraordinary loue.
2. That for me to wryte a poem of St *paules* conversion as I was determined he said wold be as if I should go wryte a book of fast & loose, esteeming *Paul* a Jugler.

Baines probably told Kyd of the Deptford entry, as Kyd refers to Marlowe's alleged 'rashness in attempting soden pryvie injuries to men' though I did 'often reprehend him for it'. Marlowe's three court appearances, and the reasons for them, show that Marlowe was gentler than many of his contemporaries, and there is no record of Kyd's being involved with any of them; Kyd saw in Baines's news a chance to condemn Marlowe in an effort to exonerate himself. He did not succeed. Kyd was not exonerated. And it was several years before criticism of Marlowe was to appear in writing again.

This new criticism was by a Puritan named Thomas Beard, in the *Theatre of Gods Judgement* (1597), and it sparked off defence of Kit with the publication of *Hero and Leander* the next year. Beard's criticisms were:

Not inferiour to any of the former in Atheisme & impiety, and equall to all in manner of punishment was one of our own nation, of fresh and late memory, called *Marlin*, by profession a scholler, brought vp from his youth in the Vniuersitie of Cambridge, but by practise a play-maker, and a Poet of scurrilitie, who by giuing too large a swinge to his owne wit, and suffering his lust to haue the full raines, fell (not without iust desert) to that outrage and extremitie, that hee denied God and his sonne Christ, and not only in word blasphemed the trinitie, but also (as it is credibly reported) wrote bookes against it, affirming our Saviour to be but a deceiuer, and *Moses* to be but a coniurer and seducer of the people, and the holy Bible but vaine and idle stories, and all religion but a deuice of pollicie. But see what a hooke the Lord put in the nosthrils of this barking dogge: It so fell out, that in London streets as he purposed to stab one whome hee ought a grudge vnto with his dagger, the other party perceiuing so auoided the stroke, that withall catching hold of his wrest, he stabbed his owne dagger into his owne head, in such sort, that notwithstanding all the meanes of surgerie that could be wrought, hee shortly after died thereof. The manner of his death being so terrible (for hee euen cursed and blasphemed to his last gaspe, and togither with his breath an oth flew out of his mouth) that it was not only a manifest signe of Gods judgement, but also an horrible and fearefull terrour to all that beheld him. But herein did the iustice of God most notably appeare, in that hee compelled his owne hand which had written those blasphemies to be the instrument to punish him, and that in his braine, which had deuised the same.

Beard's piece was garbled, even about the stabbing, which he placed in a London street, and he has Marlowe stabbing himself. Extraordinarily this picture of Marlowe is sometimes quoted, even though it bears little resemblance to the character of Marlowe in his writing, and none to what happened, including the Deptford misapprehensions. Several other Puritans took up this description in the years that followed, adding ornament that divorced it still further from fact:

We read of one *Marlin,* a *Cambridge* Scholler, who was a Poet, and a filthy Play-maker, this wretch accounted that meeke seruant of God *Moses* to be but a Coniurer, and our sweete Sauiour but a seducer and a deceiuer of the people. But harken yee braine-sicke and prophane Poets, and Players, that bewitch idle eares with foolish vanities: what fell vpon this prophane wretch, hauing a quarrell against one whom he met in a streete in London, and would haue stabd him: But the partie perceiuing his villany preuented him with catching his hand, and turning his owne dagger into his braines, and so blashpheming and cursing, he yeelded vp his stinking breath: mark this yee Players, that liue by making fooles laugh at sinne and wickednesse.

Edmund Rudierde
*The Thunderbolt of Gods Wrath against Harde-hearted
and Stiffe-necked Sinners*, 1618.

In two versions (Francis Meres *Palladis Tamia*, 1598, and Anthony a Wood, *Athenae Oxonienses*, 1691) Frizer was a rival in love for 'a certain Woman'. So whatever the inaccuracies of the descriptions of Marlowe's death, no one was accusing him of homosexuality in the seventeenth century!

But see the end of this person, which was noted by all, especially the Precisians. For it so fell out, that he being deeply in love with a certain Woman, had for his rival a bawdy serving man, one rather fit to be a Pimp, than an ingenuous *Amoretto* as *Marlo* conceived himself to be. Whereupon *Marlo* taking it to be a high affront, rush'd in upon, to stab, him, with his dagger. But the serving man being very quick, so avoided the stroke, that with all catching hold of *Marlo's* wrist, he stab'd his own dagger into his own head, in such sort, that notwithstanding all the means of surgery that could be wrought, he shortly after died of his wound.

Anthony a Wood
Athenae Oxonienses, 1691.

From Edmund Rudierde's piece of 1618 we see that Marlowe's alleged statements 'that Moses was a conjurer' or juggler, and Christ a 'seducer', were the only ones still quoted. Moses also featured in the accusations against Raleigh's circle at Cerne Abbas and later. No doubt Baines went on talking, and then interested parties for and against Marlowe's and Raleigh's circles sought out and read relevant documents, including Baines's note of 1593.

Shakespeare had read this note by the time he wrote the scenes about the burial of Ophelia in *Hamlet*. Shakespeare was to remember Marlowe in *The Tempest* at the end of his career, earlier in the *Sonnets*, and there are a number of *Faustus* quotes in the Ophelia burial scenes in *Hamlet* as well as the reference to Baines's note. This was when Hamlet talked of the 'bugs and goblins in my life', echoing Baines's 'willing them not to be afeard of bugbeares and hobgoblins'.

There are similar references in both plays to Alexander and Caesar, and to Wittenberg, where both Hamlet and Faustus had studied. Faustus's 'Mountains and hills, come, come and fall on me', becomes Hamlet's 'And, if thou prate of mountains, let them throw Millions of acres on us', which Hamlet said standing in the grave.

Both call on moving stars:

Hamlet: . . . whose phase of sorrow
Conjures the wandering stars, and makes them stand . . .

Faustus: Stand still, you ever-moving spheres of heaven,
That time may cease . . .
The stars move still, time runs, . . .
You stars reigned at my nativity . . .
Now draw up Faustus . . .

In Shakespeare's play, at the grave, Laertes said to Hamlet 'The devil take thy soul!' which is what happened to Faustus.

While some critics think Shakespeare's *Hamlet* refers to the Earl of Essex because Lord Burleigh is satirized as Polonius, there is no doubt that Shakespeare thought of Marlowe in Ophelia's burial scenes. Most probably Hamlet was just Hamlet; there had been an earlier play by Kyd, and the Danish Amleth legend was well known. Polonius/Burleigh, and Hamlet/ Marlowe in the burial scenes, were separate ingredients.

However, because Shakespeare thought of Marlowe in this way it does suggest that he might have been present at a garden burial of Marlowe.

The publication of *Hero and Leander* after Thomas Beard's

criticisms, with its introduction by Blout which obliquely alludes to such a burial setting, brought in Audrey Walsingham's name with the dedication to her of Chapman's completion of the poem. It is possible she was the subject of the 'lewde love' for whom Marlowe's rival, a serving man, slew him, according to Francis Meres in 1598 – the year of *Hero and Leander*'s publication – and the woman for whom the serving man was 'rather fit to be a Pimp' according to Anthony a Wood ninety years later. Frizer did conduct some shady deals for Lady Audrey.

The manuscript copy of 'Come Live With Me and Be My Love', coupled with Raleigh's 'Reply', which appeared in the commonplace book of the chaplain to the Earl of Pembroke, could have been given to him by Audrey, who was a friend of Mrs Thornborough (according to evidence given at the trial of the Earl and Countess of Somerset for the murder of Thomas Overbury). Marlowe of course was connected with the Pembroke household in that he had written *Edward II* for the Earl's players, but he would not necessarily have known the chaplain.

The indictment against a man called Richard Chomley by an anonymous informer should also be noted. Irreligious accusations against him are so like those imputed to Marlowe that they seem to have been standard form at the time, and not personalized.

His seconde course is to make a Ieste of the Scripture wth these fearefull horrible & damnable speeches, that Ihesus Christe was a bastarde St Mary a whore & the Anngell Gabriell a Bawde to the holy ghoste & that Christe was Iustly p[er]secuted by the Iews for his owne foolishnes that Moyses was a Iugler & Aaron a Cosoner the one for his miracles to Pharao to prove there was a god,, & the other for takinge the Earerings of the children of Israell to make a golden calfe wth many other blasphemous speeches of the devine essence of god wch I feare to rehearse This Cursed Cholmeley hath Lx therefore of his company & hee is seldome from his felowes & therefore I beeseech yor worship haue a speciall care of yor selfe in apprehendinge him for they bee resolute murderinge myndes.

However, Chomley differed in one way from Marlowe. He made accusations against *others* of atheism and machiavellianism, according to the informer. This at least demonstrates that Marlowe was not unusual in being thus accused. Some people who read about Marlowe in isolation make the mistake of thinking that atheism and machiavellianism charges were rare. According to the indictment, Chomley accused the most unlikely people of these evils.

That hee speaketh in generall all evill of the Counsell; sayenge that they are all Atheistes & Machiavillians, especially my Lord Admirall.

That hee made certen libellious verses in Comendacen of papistes & Seminary priestes very greately inveighinge againste the State, amonge wch lynes this was one, Nor may the Prince deny the Papall Crowne.

That hee had a certen booke (as hee saieth) deliverd him by Sr Robt Cecill of whom hee geveth very scandalous reporte, that hee should invite him to consider thereof & to frame verses & libells in Comendacen of constant Priests & vertuous Recusants, this booke is in Custodue & is called an Epistle of Comforte & is printed at Paris.

That he railes at Mr Topcliffe & hath written another libell Ioyntlye againste Sr Francis Drake & Iustice younge whom hee saieth hee will Couple vp together because hee hateth them alike.

That when the muteny happened after the Portingale voyage in the Strand hee said that hee repented him of nothinge more then that hee had not killed my Lord Threasorer wth his owne handes sayenge that hee could not have Done god better service, this was spoken in the hearinge of Franncis Clerke & many other Souldieurs.

That hee saieth hee doeth entirely hate the Lord Chamberleyn & hath good cause to so doe.

He does not forget Marlowe, and claims that Marlowe actually spoke about atheism to him as well as to Raleigh's circle.

It was easy for the few people who claimed to have heard atheism preached by Marlowe to do so after his death, as Marlowe could not defend himself. But against such statements should be put Marlowe's own *Doctor Faustus*. Marlowe had spoken for himself in his plays.

Due to circumstances not of his own making, Marlowe has appeared an enigmatic figure. This is not so if hearsay statements are seen in perspective, if he is placed in his period, and if his works are read without preconceived ideas.

Perhaps he achieved success too young, but as the forces which helped him to early success also caused his eclipse, one cannot be taken without the other.

He was a pioneering genius, leaving an example both as playwright and poet for others to follow. The first novelists, for example, did not achieve for their art form what Marlowe did, in his late twenties, with *Edward II* and *Doctor Faustus*.

Marlowe's life complemented his work, and it is sad if unsubstantiated hearsay statements confuse understanding of his personality.

For example, his youthful beliefs, as set out in *Tamburlaine*, inspire all lovers of beauty:

> What is beauty, saith my sufferings, then?
> If all the pens that ever poets held
> Had fed the feeling of their masters' thoughts,
> And every sweetness that inspir'd their hearts,
> Their minds, and muses on admired themes;
> If all the heavenly quintessence they still
> From their immortal flowers of poesy,
> Wherein, as in a mirror, we perceive
> The highest reaches of a human wit;
> If these had made one poem's period,
> And all combin'd in beauty's worthiness,
> Yet should there hover in their restless heads
> One thought, one grace, one wonder, at the least,
> Which into words no virtue can digest.

This is Christopher Marlowe.

Selected Bibliography

EDITIONS OF CHRISTOPHER MARLOWE'S PLAYS AND POEMS

Clarendon, ed. Tucker Brooke, Oxford 1910

Everyman's Library, ed. M. R. Ridley, London 1955

Penguin, *The Complete Plays*, ed. J. B. Steane, London 1969; *The Complete Poems*, ed. S. Orgel, London 1971

Single plays: *Doctor Faustus*, ed. John D. Jump, The Revels Plays, London 1969; *Edward II*, ed. W. Moelwyn Merchant, New Mermaid

CONTEMPORARY WORKS

Aubrey, John, *Brief Lives*

Forman, Simon, *Diaries*, ed. A. L. Rowse

Henslowe, Philip, *Diary*

Holinshed, *Chronicles, Shakespeare Sources*, ed. Professor Allardyce Nicoll & Josephine Nicoll

James I of England, *New Poems*, ed. Allan F. Westcott, Columbia University, 1911

Nashe, Thomas, *Works*, ed. R. B. MacKerrow, 1904–10

'P.F.' (translator), *The Damnable Life of Doctor John Faustus*

Plays, by Shakespeare, Kyd, Jonson, Greene, Webster

Poems, Elizabethan, ed. by E. Lucie-Smith

Stow, John, *Survey of London*

WORKS ON MARLOWE

Bakeless, John, *The Tragicall History of Christopher Marlowe*, 1942

Boas, Frederick, *Christopher Marlowe*, 1940

Hotson, L., *The Death of Christopher Marlowe*, 1925

Rowse, A. L., *Christopher Marlowe*, 1964

Wraight, A. D., *In Search of Christopher Marlowe*, 1965

BIBLIOGRAPHY

WORKS ON SHAKESPEARE

Brown, Ivor, *How Shakespeare Spent the Day; Shakespeare and the Actors,* 1970

Burgess, Anthony, *William Shakespeare,* 1970

Gibson, N. N., *The Shakespeare Claimants,* 1962

Hotson, L., *Shakespeare's Wooden O,* 1959

Quennell, Peter, *Shakespeare,* 1962

Rowse, A. L., *Shakespeare the Man,* 1974

GENERAL

J. H. Adamson & H. F. Folland, *Shepherd of the Ocean* [Raleigh], 1969

Ashton, Robert, *James I by his Contemporaries,* 1969

Bevan, Brian, *Great Seamen of England,* 1971

Brooke, Iris, *History of English Fashion,* 1968

Chambers, E. K., *The Elizabethan Stage,* various editions

Ellis-Fermor, U., *The Jacobean Drama,* 1965

Falkus, Christopher, *The Private Lives of Tudor Monarchs,* 1974

French, Peter J., *John Dee, The World of an Elizabethan Magus,* 1972

Granville-Barker, H., *Prefaces to Shakespeare,* 1927

Howell, Roger, *Philip Sidney, the Shepherd Knight,* 1968

Hurstfield, Joel, *Freedom, Corruption and Government in Elizabethan England,* 1973

Wain, John, ed. *Macbeth – Casebook Series,* 1968

Wilde, Oscar, *The Portrait of Mr W. H.,* 1889

Williams, Neville, *All the Queen's Men,* 1972

Wilson, F. P., ed. Helen Gardner, *Shakespearian and Other Studies,* 1969

Wilson, G. Knight, *The Wheel of Fire,* 1930

Yates, Frances, *The Rosicrucian Englightenment,* 1972

Index